The Bible: Dig a Little Deeper

A Guide to Accurately Interpreting the Word of God

Geoff Bennett

Sovereign World

Sovereign World Ltd
PO Box 777
Tonbridge
Kent TN11 0ZS
England

ISBN 1 85240 317 9

The publishers aim to produce books which will help to extend and build up the Kingdom of God. We do not necessarily agree with every view expressed by the author, or with every interpretation of Scripture expressed. We expect each reader to make his/her judgement in the light of their own understanding of God's Word and in an attitude of Christian love and fellowship.

Cover design by CCD, www.ccdgroup.co.uk
Typeset by CRB Associates, Reepham, Norfolk
Printed in England by Clays Ltd, St Ives plc

Dedication

To my dear wife Isobel for her encouragement and patient correcting of these pages.
Also to my elder son Stephen for his suggestions and some rephrasing.

Contents

Preface

In this book I have tried to keep the choice of words as simple as possible and, where necessary, have included explanations. I have used a few Greek words but these are spelt out in English and are used as examples. This is not an academic text book on the subject of hermeneutics (the science of the interpretation of the Bible), but a practical help based on research gathered from my years of study and lecturing.

That lovely old hymn 'Thy Word is like a garden, Lord' has as the second verse these words:

> Thy Word is like a deep, deep mine,
> And jewels rich and rare
> Are hidden in its mighty depth
> For every searcher there.

Later we sing 'Oh! May I love Thy precious Word, may I explore its mine!' I hope in this book you will find some tools to do just that, and as you get digging in the Word of God all its precious truths might be revealed to you like jewels in a mine.

I have been greatly blessed by Michael Eaton's series *Preaching through the Bible*. Similarly, I hope this book will encourage many to go on with the Lord and His Word, and will make Him known through the power of His Holy Spirit.

Introduction

God has spoken. Of that there is no doubt. In the first chapter of the book of Genesis we read *'and God said'* (v. 3). Throughout the Bible we read that God spoke. In the last book of the Bible we read *'Behold I am coming soon! Blessed is he who keeps the words of the prophecy in this book'* (Revelation 22:7). So, God wants us to understand and obey what He says.

Yes God has spoken, but the question is 'What has He said?' How is it that two people who claim to understand God, often arrive at a different meaning of **what** God has said? Why are there so many cults today all claiming they know what God has said?

The purpose of this book is to try and make some sense of what God has said; to look at ways of interpreting and understanding God's Word. This is not a technical book, but rather a general help to ordinary Christians who want to be able to read and understand God's Word better. I hope it will also be a valuable resource to leaders who want to improve their preaching and teaching.

Why do we need to learn how to interpret the Bible in the first place? Basically it's because of our sin.

> 'Sin has two main effects in the life of a human being.
>
> 1. Condemnation by God (John 3:36)
> 2. Separation from God (Isaiah 59:2)

Sin keeps the sinner out of God's presence and brings the sinner before the judgement seat. It also stops us from having a right understanding of the Bible.

But praise God! The death of His Son provides two counter effects.

1. No condemnation to those who are in Christ Jesus (Romans 8:1). This we call **justification**.
2. No separation (Romans 5:1–2). This we call **sanctification**.

Not only did Christ "put away sin" (Hebrews 9:26) and "made an end" (Daniel 9:24) of the sins of His people, they are not only freed from all condemnation, but they are also given the right of drawing near to God as purged worshippers. Sin not only means *guilt,* it also *defiles*; and the blood of Christ has not only secured *pardon*, it *cleanses*.'[1]

Note

[1] Taken from *The Doctrine of Sanctification* by A.W. Pink.

Chapter 1

A Look at the Interpreter

The Bible is a supernatural book and can only be understood by a supernatural interpreter (1 Corinthians 2:14). If your radio set is not connected to the mains power or has no batteries, you will never hear a thing! So with God's Word you must be 'connected to the power' before you can begin to hear God. Here are the requirements of being 'connected'.

1. You must be *redeemed*

It is faith in the Lord Jesus Christ that unites you to Him. Faith moves you spiritually into God's kingdom. The new birth is this first step (John 3:3). This great change comes about by the Holy Spirit's work in our lives. We move from darkness to light and from being under the power of Satan to being under the power of God (Acts 18:26). This is the effect of being justified and sanctified. How great is the joy when we know our sins are forgiven and we are part of the body of our Lord Jesus Christ – the Church!

2. You must *reverence* God

There are some who come to God and think they know better than Him, but God is Sovereign. We accept this, and we believe this. This is linked with the Lordship of Jesus Christ in our lives. Jesus said *'You call me Teacher and Lord, and rightly so for that is what I am'* (John 13:13). You will notice in verse 14 that the Lord changes this order to *'Lord and Teacher'*. To own Jesus as Lord is to put Him first in every part of your life. This shows a deep reverence for God.

3. You must *respect* His Word

We place ourselves either under the authority of the Word of God or over it. The only way to walk with God is to place ourselves under its authority; to have a respect for it, to realise it is our daily food, that which sustains us. Ezekiel was told to eat a scroll of God's Word and he would be fed. He was then to go and speak God's word to the Israelites (Ezekiel 2:8; 3:1–3). (N.B. Ezekiel did not literally eat the scroll, we take these words as a figure of speech – see chapter 21.)

4. You must *rely* on the Holy Spirit

As we believe the gospel we receive the Holy Spirit, but not always in His fullness and power (John 14:14, 17; 1 Corinthians 6:19). The promise is that the Holy Spirit will lead us into all truth, He will always glorify the Lord Jesus. Here then is a test. As we put the Bible into practice, anything that does not honour the Lord Jesus is not of God, nor in agreement with His Word.

Relying on the Holy Spirit does not mean we give up our brains or learning. God gave us intelligence and we are to use it in His service. Therefore learning is good, especially when it is learning the Bible and how to use it. The Word of God is the sword of the Spirit given to us to use. We need to be good swordsmen. The true work of the Holy Spirit will drive us to the Word of God.

5. You must *receive* the Bible as the Word of God

Some people teach that the Bible 'contains' the Word of God, but who is able to say which part is God's Word and which part is not? No one! We accept the whole Bible as the Word of God. We take more than an interest in what it says; we must be willing to spend time and effort to understand the book which is God's message to all peoples (1 Thessalonians 2:13). If you receive a letter from someone you love, you pay attention to every word written; so we do with the Word of God.

6. You must *relay* the Word to others

If you had to read a letter to a blind person, you would be careful to get it right. So, if we are to preach the Word to others we must be careful to get what we say right. If the message is to make sense to the hearers, we must not add anything or take away anything of the message itself. A preacher who only preaches the love of God and never preaches the wrath of God is preaching a one-sided message.

7. You must *rejoice* in the Word of God

Some people play about with the Bible, like some kind of religious toy, using it for spiritual entertainment. It was John Calvin, one of the great reformers, who said '[The Bible is] ... the sceptre by which the heavenly King rules His people.' This does not mean we treat the Bible like a rod of iron. The Bible is a source of light (Psalm 119:105) and it brings a richness to the soul and encouragement to us day by day in a world that is very discouraging. As we read and understand the Word our lives will deepen with joy.

> 'Faith in God is a terrific venture in the dark. I have to believe that God is good in spite of all that contradicts it in my experience. It is not easy to say that God is love when everything that happens actually gives the lie to it. Everyone's soul represents some kind of battlefield. The point for each one is whether we will hang in and say, "Though things look black. I will trust in God."'[1]

Note

1 From *Baffled to Fight Better* by Oswald Chambers. Oswald Chambers Publications Association, 1931.

Chapter 2

A Look at the Book

We have looked at the Interpreter, so now let us look at the book we are to interpret. In 1647 a number of Christian men gathered at Westminster in London and wrote a series of questions and answers about the Christian faith. We know it as the Shorter Catechism. I love the first question. 'What is the chief end of man?' And the answer is clear and simple: 'Man's chief end is to glorify God, and to enjoy Him for ever.'

The second question is this: 'What rule has God given to direct us how we may glorify and enjoy Him?' And the answer: 'The Word of God – which is contained in the Scriptures of the Old and New Testaments – is the only rule to direct us how we may glorify and enjoy Him.'

It is the Bible we are to study in order to know God and to enjoy Him. I heard in a church confession these words: 'We confess that this Word of God was not sent nor delivered by the will of man, but that holy men of God spoke as they were moved by the Holy Spirit' (see 2 Peter 1:21).

The Church of England has 39 articles of faith. Number 6 says 'Holy Scripture contains all things necessary to salvation'.

Let us look at six things about the Bible.

1. The Bible is an inspired book

This is the great principle that controls any understanding of the Bible. It cannot be ignored. Anyone coming to read the Bible and ignoring the fact that it is an inspired book is unable to know its true meaning. It is the **whole** Bible to which we come, and it is the **whole** Bible we accept as inspired. 2 Timothy 3:16 says, *'**All** scripture is God breathed.'*

What do we mean by inspired? We mean that God supernaturally influenced the writers of Scripture, so that what they wrote became divine truthfulness making an infallible (incapable of error) and sufficient rule of faith and practice. Dr B.B. Warfield said 'the writers did not work on their own initiative.' [1]

2. The Old Testament writers were inspired

Right from Exodus 7:1 God made it clear that prophets were men who spoke for Him. In the case of Jeremiah He said,

> *'Then the LORD reached out his hand and touched my mouth and said to me, "Now, I have put my words in your mouth."'*
> (Jeremiah 1:9)

We also see that the Spirit of God came upon these prophets, that God's hand was strong upon them, they received the word of God and were constrained to speak it (see Isaiah 8:11; Jeremiah 15:17; Ezekiel 1:3).

When we read what the prophets said we see that they knew God was speaking through them. The great phrase 'Thus says the Lord' or 'Hear the word of the Lord' occurs many times.

Another amazing thing we see in the prophets is the way they turn from the use of the third person to that of the first person. They suddenly begin speaking as if they were God. Isaiah chapter 3 is a good example. In the opening verses Isaiah is telling the people what the Lord Almighty is about to do, but in verse 4 we read 'I will.' The same thing is found in Amos 5:21.

3. The New Testament writers were inspired

In John 14:26 the Lord Jesus promised His disciples the Holy Spirit who would teach them all things, and remind them of everything He had said. From Pentecost and the giving of the Holy Spirit, the disciples spoke as infallible teachers of the people. They were confident that their testimony was the testimony of God (1 John 5:9–12). It then follows that if the disciples were inspired what they wrote was also inspired.

4. The written word is inspired

In the period we know as the New Testament period, i.e. the time the Lord lived and the early Church was moving out from Jerusalem with the gospel, the Jews possessed their Scriptures which we know as the Old Testament. What is amazing is that these Scriptures are quoted in the New Testament as having divine authority. The New Testament writers turn to the Old Testament to prove what they are saying is true. The Lord Jesus Himself did this and **nowhere** is it clearer than during His temptation. In Matthew 4:1–11 Jesus answers the devil with the words *'It is written'*, showing that His authority for refusing to bow to the devil was based on the Old Testament Scriptures. 'It is written' is the same as saying 'God says'. Paul says in Romans 3:2 that these Scriptures are *'the very words of God.'* We have already noted that 2 Timothy 3:16 says *'...all Scripture is God breathed.'*

5. The Bible is an inclusive book

There are some who say the Bible **contains** the Word of God and they give the impression that they alone know which are the parts that are the Word of God and which parts are not! We however accept the 39 books of the Old Testament and the 27 books of the New Testament as the Word of God. Occasionally, in various different translations, the books and chapters are not identical to the English Bible. For example I was preaching in Poland and asked the congregation to turn to Malachi chapter 4. The interpreter turned to me and said, 'We do not have Malachi chapter 4!' This meant a hurried whisper in the pulpit to find that chapters 3 and 4 in the Polish Bible are chapter 3 only. But even when this happens it is the same Bible, even though some of the chapter numbers may be different. We accept it all as the Word of God.

> *'And we also thank God continually because, when you received the word of God, which you heard from us, you accepted it not as the word of men, but as it actually is, the word of God, which is at work in you who believe.'*
>
> (1 Thessalonians 2:13)

6. The Bible is best understood by intelligent faith

As we approach the Holy Scripture it is important to note one or two things.

(a) There are difficult passages in the Bible. For example look in 2 Peter 3:15–16, where even Peter found *'some things'* of the Apostle Paul *'hard to understand.'* Praise God he did not say 'all things' but only 'some things'. He also did not say they were impossible to understand, just 'hard'!

(b) On the other hand there are those who say everything in the Bible is simple. 'All you have to do,' they say 'is believe the Bible and not explain it.' God does not ask for blind belief, but an intelligent faith.

Three things are vital to understanding the Word of God:

(a) The Bible is to be read or heard.

(b) The Bible is to be understood.

(c) The Bible is to be personally relevant to us.

It was the Lord Himself who said in Matthew 24:15, *'let the reader understand.'* And so we are to exercise our mind on what we read. In the parable of the sower, Matthew 13, the Lord says in verse 23,

'But the one who received the seed that fell on good soil is the man who hears the word and understands it.'

We need to be like the good soil.

Note

[1] Quoted by L. Berkhof in *Principles of Biblical Interpretation*, Baker House Books, 1950.

Chapter 3

A Look at How We Read the Book

As we begin to read the Bible seriously and try to understand it, we see that there are different ways of looking at it. Down through the years different groups of Christians have interpreted it in different ways. Here are five main ways in which people have looked at the Bible and tried to understand it.

1. The allegory way

An allegory is a story with a hidden meaning. Therefore instead of reading the words at face value we look all the time for some other meaning that is hidden in the story. Most books that use allegories tell you so before you begin to read so you have no problem with that. The most famous Christian allegory is *The Pilgrim's Progress* by John Bunyan.

When it comes to the Bible, people say we should look for a hidden meaning in the text. It is like saying that the Bible does not mean what it says, but we have to find a deeper meaning. Now this is very hard. Who is able to say what is plain text and what is a hidden meaning? Everyone could come up with their own completely different interpretations.

I am not saying there are **no** allegories in the Bible. They are there, but they are few and it is clear that they are allegories and not to be taken literally.

2. The devotional way

Reading the Bible devotionally, that is to feed your own soul, is the most popular way. We read it in our quiet time each day waiting for God to speak to us through His Word. There is nothing wrong with this, but it is easy to place yourself at the centre of the reading and think everything refers to you. The idea that everything in the Bible is about us and refers to us can be misleading. That this method is the most popular is proved by the number of devotional books available in Christian Bookshops. There are some preachers whose whole ministry consists of devotional preaching. This is important, but when it becomes the only way of interpreting the Bible then we are in danger. Following this way **only** can lead to the allegorising mentioned above. It can also become a substitute for expository and doctrinal preaching. If you only approach the Bible in a devotional way you can miss the great truths of the Scriptures that save you and build you up in your faith.

3. The liberal way

In the middle of the 18th century a group of men arose who thought they knew better than the Bible. They began what is called 'Higher Criticism'. They denied the supernatural, therefore Jesus did not perform any miracles. They denied Jesus was the Son of God, so His death on the cross was nothing that affected mankind. I could go on! This way of reading the Bible has done much damage to the Church and has led many people into a very low view of the Bible, so it is treated just like any other book.

Today this liberal way of thinking is very common and this teaching is to be found in many churches and Christian colleges. I like this comment from C.S. Lewis writing about people who read the Bible in a liberal way:

> 'These men ask me to believe they can read between the lines of the old texts; the evidence is their obvious inability to read the lines themselves.'[1]

4. The neo-orthodox way

'Neo' means 'to add'. If the liberal way **takes away** something from the Bible, then this is a way of reading that **adds something** to the Bible.

This group of people like to think of themselves as orthodox (that is believing the basic doctrines of the Christian faith), but they like to go further and add things. They add their own ideas ending up by denying the infallibility of the Bible. They also deny the inerrancy of Scripture and they say the Bible is contradicted by modern science. This is a rather complicated theory, but need not worry us other than to know it exists.

5. The literal way

The great preacher Charles Spurgeon was once asked by a young man if he could help him with the meaning of a verse of the Bible. 'Can you tell me what it means?' asked the young man. 'Yes,' replied Spurgeon, 'It means exactly what it says.'

Most of the Bible makes sense when it is read just as it was meant to be read, plainly and simply and taking the verses literally. This is what has happened down through the years as the Church has grown. Those who have kept the light of the gospel have read the Bible this way. We should read the Bible in a literal way, this not only makes sense but it is as God intended. We will discover more about the literal way in the next chapter.

Note

[1] From *Fern-seed and Elephants* by C.S. Lewis, published by Fount Paperbacks, 1975.

Chapter 4

A Look at the Literal Way

We saw in the last chapter that the way we should read the Bible is literally. Here we look more closely at just what this means.

1. The meaning of literal

Think how you sit down to read a book. I like to read books. When I sit down to read I intend to enjoy it. The one thing I do not do is start looking for hidden meanings, thinking the writer does not mean what he says. You would never understand what the author was saying if you approached reading like that. Unfortunately that is how many people approach the Bible. They seem to know better than God and will not accept what He says as literal. For the most part the Bible can be read quite literally. A great part of the Bible is history, so we read it as history. Some parts of the Bible are in figurative language, so we take these as figures of speech. On the whole they are obvious. In chapter 21 I will deal more with figures of speech.

So to read literally is simply to take the book as it is and read it, taking each word as it comes in the generally accepted meaning of that word. To read literally is to take each word in its socially, culturally accepted meaning. Chambers 20th Century Dictionary describes 'literal' as 'understanding words in a matter-of-fact sense'. When we communicate with each other we use words and unless we both know the general meaning of the word we have trouble. Making ourselves understood is often difficult enough, but if we 'name' things ourselves, it would be impossible to communicate. What if each person had their own name for common articles – life would be impossible!

2. The need to be understood

I have lectured in Poland for the last twelve years, but my knowledge of the Polish language is just a few words to get me understood when shopping or travelling. So when I lecture, I have to have a translator. I speak, then he speaks and hopefully the students understand. Down the years some in the Church have thought like that. They have said, 'The Bible is too hard for ordinary people to understand, so they need a translator. We the church or priests will translate it for you.' This has led to great problems with thousands who have not read the Bible for themselves, or if they have read it have needed to have the Church to interpret it for them. This is not the way God communicates with us. Praise God for Bible translators who have given us the Scriptures in many different languages so that people can read and understand for themselves.

On the other hand there is a danger when each individual reads and begins to interpret the Bible for themselves and does not acknowledge that others have different interpretations. This has led to the rise of the cults who each have their own particular interpretation of the Bible. One of the good things about meeting other believers is sharing that common understanding of the basic doctrines of the Christian faith, knowing that God has communicated His great salvation to you in the same way as He has done to others.

3. God's chosen way

God chose words to communicate His message, first spoken and then written. Ravi Zacarahias says 'In the beginning was the Word not a video or our feelings.' So knowing the literal meaning of words is vital to understanding the Bible and making the message known. I have heard it said, 'It shows a great command of the English language to be simple!' I understand this to mean being uncomplicated in our language, using plain words to make ourselves understood. So as we sit down to read the Scriptures we do not look for hidden meanings, nor do we take words and change them into something else. We take them literally.

4. Not being a slave

Reading the Bible literally does not mean we have to be a slave to the meaning of each word. It is often the meaning of the sentence or paragraph that matters. For example, someone might say 'I am dying to meet you.' We do not take the word 'dying' literally to mean the end of life, but simply they are eager to meet us.

Nor does reading literally mean things have to be flat or boring. Paul emphasises this thought in 2 Corinthians 3:6.

> *'He has made us competent as ministers of a new covenant – not of the letter but of the Spirit, for the letter kills, but the Spirit gives life.'*

We do not ignore the meaning of each individual word, neither do we get into such a narrow frame of mind that we give it one meaning and one meaning only. The word in one context might have a slightly different meaning from when it appears in another context.

One of my daughters, when younger, used to have a rather annoying habit. She was what I call a 'literalist'. My wife or I would make a statement, or ask her to do something and she would pick up on the words and start to examine them. She was not being deliberately difficult, it seemed to be her nature. In the same way the detailed examination of words on their own, out of context, can kill communication, and the one thing we want to do is communicate the Bible to those who hear us preach and teach. In the next chapter we move from a literal interpretation of the Bible to a cultural interpretation.

Chapter 5

A Look at Culture

When it comes to understanding the Bible I often tell my students 'Culture is everything.' In fact when it comes to understanding anyone from a different country we cannot ignore their culture. I have had the opportunity of travelling across the world. In my teens I had to serve two years in the Army like most men of my age. I travelled to Singapore by air. It took nine days, we often stopped to refuel and then the aeroplane broke down. We went first to Cyprus, then to Bahrain where we stayed over two days waiting for the plane to be repaired. Then Karachi, Goa and Calcutta before eventually arriving in Singapore. This was my first time abroad and first time flying. I began to see other cultures, that people lived differently from me. I had read about it, but here I was experiencing it.

1. What is culture?

By culture we mean all the ways people live, their methods, manners, tools, the institutions with which a given people or tribe or nation carry on their existence. Unless we know the culture in which the Bible was written, we will not be able to understand it.

Culture is generally divided into two parts.

(a) **Material**. This means things like tools, weapons, objects, houses, clothing that people use everyday in order to live. The Scriptures are filled with references to these things. You do not have to read far into the Bible before you read of 'eating' (Genesis 3:6) and 'clothing' (Genesis 3:21). A city is mentioned in Genesis 4:17; a harp and flute in 4:21; tools 4:22.

In the New Testament we know that the lamps used were Grecian lamps which were quite small and did not hold much oil (Matthew 25:1). Bread was baked in thin sheets over small earthen ovens fuelled by grass (Matthew 6:30).

(b) **Social**. This means the customs and practices of people. Birth, puberty, marriage, burial rituals. It means the political structures of a people and how they governed themselves. By the time of the New Testament there were three political systems. There was powerful Rome which conquered all the lands around the Mediterranean; King Herod ruling Judea with the permission of Rome; then the Jewish Parliament, called the Sanhedrin, who kept an eye on the religious life of the country. Social culture is about politics, the legal system, religion and the economics of any group of people.

2. Culture helps us understand

Words, sentences and expressions only have meaning in terms of a culture. The cultural approach to the Bible is necessary and essential if we hold to a literal understanding of Scripture, but there can be a danger in being held too close to culture. Some scholars explain passages in the Old Testament as only having a cultural interpretation. In other words, they tend to explain it away by appealing to culture and say it was only relevant for those people at that time.

3. Culture is only a guide

The idea of the culture principle is not to do away with biblical religion or theology, but to serve as a guide to the proper understanding of the Bible. It does save us from fanciful interpretations because its basis is the interpretation of facts.

4. Culture leads us to look at biblical geography

Maps are very important to those who travel. It would be very difficult without them. If you want to travel in your 'mind' throughout the Bible lands, then you need a map. For instance, it is very important in understanding Scripture to know about mountains.

You will remember the parable of the Good Samaritan. It begins *'A man went down from Jerusalem to Jericho'* (Luke 10:30). If you know your geography, then you will know that Jerusalem is high in the mountains about 800 metres above sea level, so to travel to Jericho you have to go downhill. Some knowledge of rivers, plains, the seasons, crops etc. will also aid us in understanding the Bible.

The Bible is a book of the Middle East. Abraham travelled from Ur of the Chaldees to the land of Canaan. The route he chose was along what is known as the Fertile Crescent. It can be traced looking at a map of the Middle East. Starting at Egypt go up through Israel and then bending over to the right (in the shape of a crescent), down to the Persian Gulf. This crescent is rich in water, so it was the centre of farming and the path which the trade routes followed.

Egypt plays a big part in the forming of the nation Israel. It was here that the Exodus under Moses took place. To follow their progress as they leave Egypt and make their way through the desert to Canaan is rewarding.

Most of the centre of activity in the Bible is Palestine. This is a small land only about 300/400 kilometres long and between 50 to 80 kilometres wide. For the Christian it is the centre of history.

Looking at a cross section of Palestine we can divide it into four sections.

(a) **The Coastal Plain.** This is about 200 kilometres long and extends from Lebanon in the north to the Negev desert in the south. There is one mountain on the coast, Carmel made famous by Elijah in 1 Kings 18.

(b) **The Western Hills**. This is a range of hills and mountains that run down the centre of the country from northern Galilee to Sinai. The mountains of Lebanon, famous for its cedar trees, are in the north. Lower Galilee is a range of hills about 600 metres high. It is one of the parts of the land that is mentioned little in the Old Testament. There are two famous plains here – Jezreel and Megiddo. In the centre there are the cities of Samaria, Shiloh, Bethel and Shechem. This is the part we know as Samaria. To the south is Judah and the cities of Jerusalem, Bethlehem and Hebron. This area is very mountainous and isolated.

(c) **The Rift Valley**. This starts in the foothills of Mount Hermon. The Jordan river starts here and flows into the Sea of Galilee, a fresh water lake (also called the sea of Chinnereth in Numbers 34:11, later changed to Gennesaret in Luke 5:1 and also called the Sea of Tiberias in John 6:1 after the town built on the western shore). It is 206 metres below sea level. Around the lake were many cities and in Bible times Josephus (a Jewish historian) estimated 150,000 people lived around the lake. This is the scene of the northern ministry of the Lord. The River Jordan winds its way slowly south passing the city of Jericho and empties into the Dead Sea. This is the lowest place on earth –391 metres below sea level. It is called 'dead' because it has no outlet and the only water to leave is by evaporation. The salt in the sea is so strong that you can float on the water without sinking. The Rift Valley continues south to the desert of the Arabah.

(d) **The Eastern Hills**. This area is known as Transjordan. In the north are what we know as the Golan Heights. This area is fertile because it has four rivers – the Yarmuk, Jabbok, Arnon, and Zered. But as you travel east it becomes desert. South is Gilead and Edom and Moab.

Chapter 6

A Look at History

Having looked at geography which is an important part of our knowledge of culture, we must also look at the other major part of culture – that is history.

1. History is part of *interpretation*

Somewhere today in the Middle East someone is digging into the past. We have much to thank the archaeologists for who spend their time digging into the earth, sometimes very slowly and over many years, to find the past. From clay tablets and monuments, from inscriptions on rocks and in caves to pieces of papyri (the earliest form of paper) and from historical documents like the writings of Josephus (mentioned in chapter 5). Little by little, line by line the archaeologist reconstructs ancient history. Understanding the Bible would be difficult if we did not have all this material to call upon to give light on the ancient world.

2. History is part of *investigation*

Genesis is made much clearer by all the work in Mesopotamia (which means 'the land between the rivers' – the rivers being the Tigris and Euphrates). Many books have been written on this period of Bible history. Studies in Egyptian history make Exodus easier to understand. Many of the events in the life of Joseph are helped by the archaeologist. Diggings have taken place in Rome, Greece, Palestine, Arabia etc. These help us understand the gospels and the New Testament. Investigating history helps us understand the political intrigues and the wars we read about in the Bible. An awareness of these current events helps us to understand the prophetic books.

3. History is part of our *intelligence*

The Word of God was written in an historical setting, and without a knowledge of history the Bible does not make sense. It is like trying to read a novel about the American civil war with no idea that the north and south of America ever had a war. To understand an author's work we need to know something about the setting in which he writes. The Bible's setting is history. All the author's writings are influenced by the time, place and circumstances in which he writes. It is good to ask the following questions when you approach a book of the Bible.

▶ Who is the author?

This is not always easy because some books of the Bible do not tell us who wrote them, but there are clues. John's Gospel is a good example. In John 13:23; 21:7; 21:20 we find the expression 'the disciple whom Jesus loved'. Here we can play detective and work out that it is John himself who wrote the Gospel. The more you know about the author the more you can begin to understand the book.

▶ Who is the speaker?

We sometimes read the words of people other than the author. It is good to note these. Also the prophets sometimes speak their own words as well as speaking on behalf of God.

▶ Who are the readers?

Whilst the Bible is God's Word to mankind, many of the individual books were written to people. The prophets wrote to Judah or Israel. Most of the New Testament was written to churches or individuals. Luke wrote to a man called Theophilus (Luke 1:1–4; Acts 1:1) All we know about him is that his name means 'loved by God' and that he was the Christian who received these two books of Luke. Knowing about the situation in Corinth helps us understand the two letters of Paul to the Corinthians.

Chapter 7

A Look at Appreciation

We come now to the third important aspect of biblical interpretation. We first looked at both literal and cultural aspects. I call this part **appreciation**.

I once was talking to a friend who is quite learned in the Scriptures, about Matthew 24:29:

> *'Immediately after the distress of those days "the sun will be darkened, and the moon will not give its light; the stars will fall from the sky, and the heavenly bodies will be shaken."'*

In this verse the Lord Jesus is quoting Isaiah 13:10 and 34:4. I asked my friend what he thought this verse meant. He said that it meant the falling of political figures from their positions of power. I then said to him, 'How do you know that?' He started to answer me, but could not give an adequate justification for his interpretation. That is what I mean by **appreciation** – that we are able to justify the grounds for our interpretations. Just as Peter says believers must be able to give a reason for the hope that they have in Christ (1 Peter 3:15), so as we interpret the Bible we must be able to give reasons for what we say. Otherwise we can make the Bible say anything we want.

I was converted in Singapore during my two years army service through an Army Scripture Reader. He regularly took a few of us with him when he visited the barracks to evangelise. Someone once asked him where God came from. With a twinkle in his eye, he turned to his Bible, which in those days was the Authorised Version published in 1611. The man read for himself Habakkuk 3:3 which says, *'God came from Teman.'* If you look up 'Teman' in a Bible dictionary you will see it means 'south'. Of course he was using the Scriptures out of context, for we know God did not come from anywhere – He is eternal. But the Scripture Reader used the soldier's simple question in order to witness to him.

Bernard Ramm in his excellent book *Protestant Biblical Interpretation* (W.A. Wilde Company, 1956) says that our interpretation of the Bible must be 'critical' and goes on to explain, 'by critical we mean that any interpretation of Scripture must have **adequate justification**.'

He further says that,

1. 'It may be a **lexical** justification. We may quote lexicons or word-studies.
2. It may be a **grammatical** justification which will rest upon evidence supplied by standard Hebrew or Greek grammars.
3. It may be a **theological** justification: e.g. we may appeal to the general teaching of Calvinism to interpret some particular passage, e.g. Hebrews 6.
4. It may be a **cultural** justification. We may argue that such-and-such was the practice among the Jews at the time of Christ as witnessed by the writings of rabbis. For example, Sir William Ramsey argues that Paul's advice that women should have long hair and wear a veil refers to the complete veiling of women as is practised in Islamic countries today, and that prostitutes and others like them were either unveiled or had shaven heads.
5. It may be a **geographical** interpretation. Much of the understanding of Joshua's Long Day depends upon adequate geographical information.'

If we do not have the right measure of justification that we desire, then we should always admit our lack of understanding and say that our interpretation is a theory.

Bernard Ramm goes on to say,

> 'Thus the critical approach stands in definite opposition to all interpretations determined arbitrarily, dogmatically and speculatively.'

▶ Arbitrarily

That is 'off the top of our heads' or any thing we happen to think it means.

▶ Dogmatically

Some churches have what we call a 'dogma'. It means a settled opinion. A doctrine laid down by an authority. That particular church may declare that this is the only interpretation and everyone else has to slavishly follow it whether it is the right interpretation or not. Sometimes you meet people who are very dogmatic in their character and if you ask them to justify their dogma they get hot under the collar and trouble often follows. I like to keep away from this kind of person!

▶ Speculatively

Some people might speculate about all kinds of things, but when it comes to interpreting the Bible we are not to guess.

The one thing we have to guard against is having a highly personal interpretation. Here is an example: I used to lecture in a Bible College. I had been giving an explanation of a verse of Scripture to one of the students in the class. It was clear the explanation I had given was not what she wanted to hear. As I finished she said, 'Well I believe it means so and so.' Her whole basis for interpreting the verse her way was her belief. She ignored the very important rule that our interpretation must have adequate grounds. Something is clearly wrong when the Holy Spirit appears to give one person one interpretation and a different interpretation to another person. I think we need to realise we are all human and subject to human frailties. However, that does not mean to say that with study we cannot know the main themes of God's Word.

Chapter 8

A Look at an Interpreter's Tools

I am quite a keen 'do-it-yourself' person. For many years I have tackled various jobs around the house. Life has got easier in the 'do-it-yourself' field, because of the new tools that are available When I first started I had a hammer, a screwdriver, and a saw. For some jobs that is all I would need. But for more complicated jobs I needed better tools. Today there are many tools available that help in the work.

It is like that in understanding the Bible. If you have just your Bible, then it can be quite difficult to understand certain things like culture, geography and history. Things are mentioned in the Bible and you might have no idea what they are, so you turn to your tools. These are books written by experts in language, history and geography.

1. Language

The Old Testament was originally written in Hebrew, except for Ezra 4:8, 6:19, 7:12–27; Jeremiah 10:11, and Daniel 2:4, 7:28 which are in Aramaic. Aramaic is similar to Hebrew and written with the same characters.

The New Testament was written in Greek with just a few words in Aramaic. The Greek used is what we know as 'common' Greek – the everyday Greek of the street and marketplace. It was spread by the army of Alexander the

Great. As they moved East to conquer, Alexander left garrisons of soldiers who married local women and settled down, so the common or *koine* (the Greek word for 'common') Greek spread. About the year 250 BC in the town of Alexandria in Egypt the Old Testament was translated into Greek. This is called the Septuagint (abbreviated to LXX) which means 70 because 70 scholars translated it.

The fact that you may not be able to read Hebrew or Greek yourself need not worry you, because today there are many excellent tools to help us understand the text of the Bible. The essential tools are listed below:

▶ Concordance

A concordance is a list of all the words in the Bible and the places they occur. A meaning is given at the start of each word. There are two main ones published: Young and Strong. I prefer Young's because of the analytical section at the back.

Here is an example: Jesus said to Nicodemus in John 3:3 *'You must be born again.'* Looking in Young's at the word 'again' (page 19) we see there are seven words in the Greek for 'again'. Two of these are used in John chapter 3 in verses 3 and 7. The word is *anõthen* which means 'from above'. If you then turn to the back of Young's to the Index-Lexicon of the New Testament (page 59) and find *anõthen*, you will see listed five different translations: 1. 'Again' used once; 2. 'from above' used five times; 3. 'from the beginning' used once; 4. 'from the very first' used once, and 5. 'the top' used three times. You can then find these references and see how the word is used in different passages.

▶ Word dictionary

An ordinary dictionary is useful for Bible study, but better is a dictionary of New Testament words. The most common is that by W.E. Vine. This sets out each word in the New Testament in an 'anglicised' form (Greek written using English letters) and has a detailed explanation about the word. You can learn much from the use of this dictionary. At the back there are some additional notes and a Greek word index.

▶ Interlinear Greek–English New Testament

This useful book sets out the Greek text of the New Testament and underneath an English translation (word for word). At the side is the text of the English New Testament. Here you can see the position of the word in the sentence. As you may know the word order in Greek sentences is quite different from that in English.

▶ Bible dictionary

These are used just like a word dictionary, but give all the main characters, places, books, articles etc. of the Bible. They generally start with Aaron and end with Zuzim. There is a write up on each entry and some are quite extensive. This is a must for any serious student of the Bible.

2. Geography

There are many good atlases of the Bible, giving detailed maps of both the Middle East and all its lands. Often they include the journeys of the children of Israel, the allocation of the tribes of Israel and the separating of the two kingdoms (Judah and Israel). In the New Testament maps we can see the Lord's journeys, the missionary journeys of Paul, and many other interesting features.

3. History

Today you can buy many books on the history of the Bible. Some cover either the Old or the New Testament, others include both. These books will give you an understanding of the world outside the Bible and put it in the context of Bible history. One of the historical sections that is most useful is what we call the 'Inter-testament period' – the 400 years between Malachi and Matthew. It is here we see the rise of

Greek culture and the Roman Empire. This period sets the scene for the New Testament.

4. Bible commentaries

Most serious Bible students have a commentary or two. These fall into two main categories. There are complete commentaries of the whole Bible which set out to be comment on the whole Bible and therefore some of the entries are rather brief. I often find these a little frustrating. I might turn to a passage I want to study and find the commentary has no entry for these verses at all! But, on the whole, the ones I have are very good and helpful. The other kind is the 'one book' commentary. These can be fuller and give much more time to explaining the text.

A word of warning about commentaries. There is no substitute for digging into the Bible yourself. Aim to read the passage you are studying thoroughly yourself and perhaps write an outline, drawing out what the passage says to you. Ask God to make His word known to you. After you have done this, then look in the commentary which should confirm that you are on the right lines and might open your mind for further study. A second word of warning. Do not stay with one man. We all have our favourite commentaries, but to follow just one man cannot give you a wide view of Scripture. If you are able, obtain different commentaries by different authors.

5. The computer

Today the computer has made a difference to Bible study. There are various tools that can be bought quite cheaply to aid our study.

► Bible search software

This is a program that searches for a Bible verse or part of a verse. You only have to enter in a word and up come all the verses containing that word. They allow you to make notes and to print out the verses you have chosen.

▶ Bible CDs

It is possible to buy CDs with many versions of the Bible on them. Some also contain Strong's Concordance, Vine's Dictionary of New Testament Words and some commentaries. The commentaries tend to be older ones due to copyright, but they can be very useful. Whilst the computer has speeded up Bible study and has many useful tools, again it is no substitute for reading the Bible itself.

Chapter 9

A Look at Words

As we come to the text of the Bible we see that it is made up of words, words become sentences, sentences become paragraphs, paragraphs become chapters and chapters become books.

1. Chapters and verses

It is interesting to note that the original languages of the Bible (Hebrew and Greek with a little Aramaic) had no chapter or verse divisions. The divisions can be very useful for working our way around the Bible, but at times they can also be a hindrance.

It was generally accepted that a man called Cardinal Hugo divided the Bible into chapters around 1250 AD. It has since come to light that the work was done by Stephen Langton Archbishop of Canterbury around 1227 AD. In 1445 Mordecai Nathan put in the verse divisions of the Old Testament and in 1551 Robert Stephens the New Testament. As Bernard Ramm comments 'We could forgive them for thinking they "nodded off" whilst doing it', because they made so many mistakes.

Some of the new translations help us to work out the context of Bible passages better than the Authorised Version because they divide up the sections. For instance: the end of Exodus 5 runs on into chapter 6; Joshua chapter 6 starts in

5:13; Isaiah chapter 53 starts in 52:13; 1 Corinthians chapter 2:1–5 seems to belong to the end of chapter 1; 1 Peter 2:1–3 likewise. These are but a few examples and there are many, many more.

2. Punctuation

Hebrew for many centuries was without punctuation and had no vowels. During the 7th century AD a vowel system was introduced. Greek also was written without punctuation. You can see that many of the manuscripts in the British Museum not only have no chapter or verse numbers and no punctuation, but no space between the words either. Imagine trying to translate that! Remember that there are no original manuscripts of the Bible. All we have available are copies. And as people copied more punctuation came into the manuscripts.

Generally we accept the present-day punctuation, but people do change it and it can change the meaning of the text. For instance:

The Jehovah's Witness Bible the Twentieth Century Version has in Luke 23:43 this punctuation: 'Truly I say to you today, you shall be with me in Paradise.' Can you see the comma after the word 'today'? This allows an interpretation that places no time limit upon what the Lord said to the thief on the cross. If you check most translations it reads like this, 'Truly I say to you, today you shall be with me in Paradise', meaning that the thief had instant access to Paradise. The latter makes better sense.

You will note changes in punctuation between modern versions. Some of these can be helpful, others not. Most are minor changes and we would not fall out over them, but where the change affects the basic doctrines of the Christian Church we must be careful.

3. Words

Think of words as bricks in a wall. The wall needs the bricks in order to become a wall. So words make up sentences. The sentence needs the words to become a sentence. We speak to each other in sentences, that is the way we understand one another.

We may study words themselves

This is called **etymology** – it means the way words are formed and their sense developed. This is best done with a lexicon and dictionary. As we investigate words we begin to understand their meaning. This does not mean that individual words are more important that the sentence, but we have to start somewhere in our understanding.

- Here is an Old Testament example:
  Consider the Hebrew words *kopher* (ransom); *kippurim* (redemption); *kappreth* (atonement or Mercy-seat). If we investigate them we see they come from one root *kaphar,* which means 'to cover' and contains the idea of a redemption or atonement brought about by a certain covering. In the Old Testament this was the blood of an animal. In the New Testament it is the precious blood of our Lord Jesus Christ.

- Now a New Testament example:
  We all know the word 'church'. But church as such is not a Bible word. It comes from the Anglo-Saxon word *cirche* which was changed in Middle English to *chirche* and so today has become 'church'. This word comes from the Greek word *kyriakon* meaning 'the Lord's House'. I think that is why we often think of church buildings as the Lord's House or sanctuary. The Greek word in the New Testament is *ekklesia* – made up of two words: *ek* – 'out of'; and *klesis* – 'a calling'. Put together *ekklesia* means 'called out'. We could best translate it as 'assembly' or 'congregation'.

Many Bible words are made up of other words and it is good to look at the root of these words as they do help our understanding.

We study words by comparing them with other words

This is best done with a concordance and here Young's Analytical Concordance is useful. We can see how many times the word is used and which writers of the Bible used it. Think of the word 'spirit'. It can be used for evil spirit, human spirit, a proper inward attitude and the Holy Spirit. Likewise 'soul' is used for a person, enthusiasm (something done from the heart), the spiritual and the important part of a being.

We can study words that are synonyms

Synonyms are words that have the same meaning or the same sense of meaning. There are books available on Synonyms of the Old Testament (Girdlestone) and Synonyms of the New Testament (Trench).

- Here are two verses which are examples:
  Matthew 20:21 says,

  '"What do you want?" he asked. She said, "Grant that one of these two sons of mine may sit at your right and the other at your left in your kingdom."'

  Mark 10:37 reads rather differently,

  'They replied, "Let one of us sit at your right hand and the other at your left in your glory."'

In Matthew we read 'kingdom' and in Mark 'glory'. These two words are synonyms, they carry the same meaning in both these verses.

Similarly, in Matthew 18:9 we see the words *'enter life'* and in Mark 9:47 we see *'enter the kingdom of God'*. Here life is a synonym for the kingdom of God.

Words can be studied looking at their history

Most words have a history or a historical and cultural reference. Hebrews 5:7 in the New International Version says,

> *'During the days of Jesus' life on earth, he offered up prayers and petitions with loud cries and tears to the one who could*

> *save him from death, and he was heard because of his reverent submission.'*

The Revised Standard Version reads *'prayers and supplications'*. The word 'supplication' carries the idea of a person bringing an olive branch to a king or important person. As we come to God we come in supplication, not bringing an olive branch which spoke of peace, but through the blood of Christ which is our access to the Father.

In Matthew 5:41 we read,

> *'If someone forces you to go one mile, go with him two miles.'*

The Greek text here has a Persian word which means 'to press into service as a courier for the royal post'. The Romans adopted this custom. So we can see how interesting it is to look at a word historically. It brings light to the word and opens up many areas of meaning.

Chapter 10

A Look at Tenses

In this chapter we continue to look at words. There is one thing that differs in many languages and that is the order in which words appear in a sentence. In some languages this is very important, in others it is not so important. This is what we call **grammar**. Grammar has certain principles which dictate how words should be arranged in order to make a meaningful sentence. It helps us greatly to have some understanding of nouns (the name of a person, place or thing), verbs (action words), adjectives (words that describe nouns), adverbs (words that describe verbs), prepositions (words placed before a noun or a pronoun to mark some relation), and pronouns (a word used instead of a noun) etc.

1. Tense

One of the most important things in grammar is the **tense** of the words. Tense is generally about time. This gives us a clue as to when things happen, e.g. 'Tomorrow I am going to church.' This is describing an event in the future, because tomorrow has not yet come, so we know this is the future tense. The basic tenses are past, present and future. We also have simple, imperfect and perfect tenses and each one of these can be applied to past, present and future.

Bernard Ramm[1] gives a good illustration in John 1:1, *'In the beginning was the Word.'* 'Was' is in the imperfect tense.

The imperfect tense implies a previous state and its continuance. If John 1:1 were interpreted to bring out the full force of the imperfect it would be translated: 'In the beginning the Word had been existing and is still existing.' The tense of the word highlights a theological point – the eternal existence of the Son. He was already existing before the dawn of creation.

The Greek New Testament has a tense that is quite common, but not easy to translate in the English. It is called the **aorist**. It expresses simple past time with no implications of continuance, repetition or the like. Bagster in his Greek dictionary puts the aorist like this – 'strictly the expression of a momentary or transient action'.[2] For example, John 1:14 says *'And the Word became flesh.'* The word 'became' is an aorist, which means the completion of an event in historical time. This tells us that at one point in time Christ became a man.

An excellent example of the aorist tense occurs in Ephesians 4:22–24. We read,

> *'You were taught, with regard to your former way of life, to put off your old self.'* (Ephesians 4:22)

This verse reads as if it is something we are to do, as if we have the power to do it, to take off our old self and put on the new self. Yet the tense of the words 'put off' is aorist and that means it is something that has already been done once and will not be repeated. What Paul is saying is that when we trusted Christ, everything we were was stripped away and we are now new creatures in Christ. This is something Christ does for us, we are to live in the light of this truth.

2. Modern versions

There are many modern versions of the Bible, some better than others. One of the good things resulting from the modern translations is that the tenses have been refined. For instance, if you read the Authorised Version of Hebrews 1:1, it says *'God who at sundry times and in divers manners spake . . .* '. The Greek here is aorist participle and should be translated 'God having spoken' or as we see in the New International Version *'In the past God spoke . . .* '. What is vital is the next verse, *'but in these last days he has spoken to us by his Son . . .* '. So we see what the Bible is saying here. God began speaking in the Old Testament, but He did not end there, He continued in the New Testament and finished all He had to say in His Son.

Notes

1 Bernard Ramm, *Protestant Biblical Interpretation.* W.A. Wilde Company, 1956.

2 *Analytical Greek Lexicon.* Samuel Bagster & Son, London, 1841.

Chapter 11

A Look at Context

I once had a colleague who worked in another office some miles away. Occasionally she had to telephone me. People used to laugh at her because she always started her conversation in the middle of what she wanted to say. I think as she started to dial the number she began saying what was in her mind, then as the connection was made she just continued talking at the place she was up to! It was very confusing. As I listened, I could not understand at first what she was talking about. In other words, I could not grasp the context of what she was saying.

The Bible is like that. If you do not know the context then you will have great difficulty in understanding what the writer is saying. So here is a golden rule:

Context is everything

The context may be described as the parts of a passage that go before and come after a particular text, and which help us understand its true meaning. The following saying is very well known. I don't know who said it first, but it is worth noting. 'A text out of context is a pretext.' A pretext is a reason put forward to alter the true meaning.

All individual words have a meaning. But it is only when we put them into sentences that we know what the full meaning is. A child learning to speak often picks up single words and uses them in many different ways. A two-year-old we met recently had learnt the word 'zebra', and how we laughed at some of his uses of it. 'What do you want for tea Joel?' 'Zebra,' he replied. We had no idea what he meant. To understand context takes more than a sentence or two. We must study the content of the whole passage.

So as we come to the Bible we realise that we cannot pick up an isolated sentence or a text and fully understand it. We must take it in its context. If we take a text on its own we can make it say anything – that is people arrive at varying interpretations. This is how many of the cults operate. They pick up a text here and a text there and use them out of context.

Here are a few examples of the way things can be taken out of context:

1. *'Hear the church'* (Matthew 18:17) is not an instruction to the laity (so-called non-ordained members of the congregation) to submit their judgements to the clergy (so-called ordained members of the congregation). The context shows the local congregation must decide the issue when a sinning brother refuses to listen to another.
2. Wilfred Kuhrt in his book *Interpreting the Bible* (Grace Publications Trust, 1982) tells this story:

   'I came across a laughable example a few years ago in India. The offender was a very able and greatly used pastor/evangelist and he had, moreover, three years of Bible school behind him. I was therefore all the more disconcerted when I observed his method. He was speaking to a group of pastors who had been gathered together for a few days of quiet retreat. In Anglo-Indian vocabulary whenever you are away from home or from your headquarters you are on "camp".

   So our preacher friend thought of us as being on camp and then proceeded to look up the word "camp" in a concordance. He selected ten uses of the word stretching from Exodus to Revelation which appeared to him to suit his purpose and then described to us what he thought would characterise our time spent together in conference. [This, by the way, is a dubious way of using a concordance.] On the basis of Exodus 32:17–18 he told us that our camp should be characterised by singing, ignoring the context which makes it plain that the singing on that occasion was deplorable and lascivious (undisciplined, unruly). In other words, precisely the kind of song one would least expect to hear in a gathering of ministers of the gospel.'

3. In Luke 15:3–32 many have wondered who the ninety-nine sheep left in the wilderness are because they are described as 'just persons who need no repentance', or who the 'elder son' who complained at the generous treatment of his brother was. These wonderings ignore the key to this passage found in verses 1 and 2. Here we have three parables that were spoken, not to the disciples but to the Lord's enemies. The parables were spoken in reply to the Pharisees and scribes complaining about the Lord eating with sinners. The three parables are the Lord's justification for His eating with sinners and are parables about sinners finding the Saviour. They are nothing to do with backslidden Christians.
4. In 2 Peter 2:22 a Proverb (26:11) is quoted, *'...a dog returns to his own vomit.'* Some see this as believers who lose their salvation, but if we look at the context we see it has to do with false teachers.

How do we find the context?

I would suggest three ways:

▶ The Bible itself

We are dealing with an inspired book. Our understanding of sin, redemption and salvation are understood within the whole of Scripture. All the doctrines that come out of Scripture are placed within the whole plan of God.

The specific book of the Bible itself

Whether the book is in the Old Testament or the New will give a clue as to where to start. We would treat a chapter from Jeremiah differently from one from Hebrews. We also have to look at the book itself: what is its intent? What is the writer wanting to say? This gives us a clue to the meaning of a particular passage within the book. Matthew sets out to show that Jesus is the Messiah. John in his gospel seeks to show that Jesus is the Divine Son of God. 'The better we know the theme of a book, the motivation of the author, the goals intended, the better we can handle the individual passages and sentences.'[1]

The specific passage of the Bible itself

Always ask yourself: 'What has gone before and what follows?' In this way you will be aware of the need to take in the context of the passage. Remember whilst chapter numbers and verse numbers are very useful they can hinder us in finding the context. It is often good to compare different versions of the Bible and always follow the golden rule: **interpret according to the context.**

Note

1 Bernard Ramm, *Protestant Biblical Interpretation*. W.A. Wilde Company, 1956.

Chapter 12

A Look at Divisions

We started this section by looking at words, and then looked at the context of the words. Now we look at the Bible as literature.

One of the good things about living in a city is that we can have access to our local library where books can be borrowed free of charge for up to three weeks at a time. When I walk in and look at the shelves I see row after row of books, thousands of them, all shapes and sizes, some now in other languages. Where do I begin? It's quite easy if you know the system. All the books are in their own category. You look under the kind of book you want. It is no good going to the crime section if you want a dictionary. So each is under its heading in its place. It's just a case of knowing what you want.

The Bible is no different. There are different kinds of books in the Bible. Among the 66 we have: History; Law; Narrative; Songs; Poetry; Parables; Biographies; Letters; Prophecy; Apocalyptic. We need to be careful not to be too exact as prophecy can also be found in the poetry, and poetry can be found in the history etc.

Basically the Old Testament has three main sections:

1. History – 17 books
2. Poetry – 5 books
3. Prophecy – 17 books

▶ History

The first five books of Moses are known by the Jews as the Torah or Law. That leaves 12 other books that we call history. They are: Joshua, Judges, Ruth, 1–2 Samuel, 1–2 Kings, 1–2 Chronicles, Ezra, Nehemiah and Esther.

▶ Poetry

Poetry is contained in Job, Psalms, Proverbs, Ecclesiastes and Song of Solomon. They are often called the 'Wisdom Books'.

▶ Prophecy

These books are divided into **major** and **minor** prophets; not because the major prophets are more important than the minor ones, but because of the length of the books. The **major prophets** are Isaiah, Jeremiah (including Lamentations), Ezekiel and Daniel. The **minor prophets** are Hosea, Joel, Amos, Obadiah, Jonah, Micah, Nahum, Habakkuk, Zephaniah, Haggai, Zechariah and Malachi.

The New Testament also has three main sections:

1. History – 5 books
2. Letters – 21 books
3. Prophecy – 1 book

▶ History

These books are Matthew, Mark, Luke, John and Acts.

▶ Letters (also called Epistles)

There are thirteen by Paul which are Romans, 1 and 2 Corinthians, Galatians, Ephesians, Philippians, Colossians, 1 and 2 Thessalonians, 1 and 2 Timothy, Titus and Philemon. In addition there is the letter to the Hebrews (the author is unknown), James, 1 and 2 Peter, 1, 2 and 3 John, and Jude.

▶ Prophecy

The book of Revelation.

All the information you need to get an overview of the books is a good Bible Handbook, or a survey book of the Old and New Testaments, or an introduction to the Old and New Testaments.

As we look at individual books we can see generally they fall into a literary category. That helps us in our interpretation. Whilst there are general principles for interpreting the Bible, it is good to look at each book in its literary category as a guide to interpretation. It is good to recognise that the Spirit of God chose different types of literature to express the mind of God. How boring if every book in the Bible came from the same literary mould.

So as we read the book as a whole we must take note as to its type of literature. We do not read poetry as prose, or history as prophecy, although there may be prophetic parts in the history books.

It is worth mentioning here that we cannot be too rigid when we come to look at the literary categories. These categories can merge with one another. We find that prophecy is very commonly written in poetic terms. Both the Gospels and letters contain prophecy about the end times (known as apocalyptic). Parables are found in many parts of the Bible.

Chapter 13

A Look at Cross-references

Understanding the Bible as one

It is important to know that the Bible is one, even though it has two main parts the Old and New Testaments, and is made up of 66 individual books. It took around 1,500 years to write and has at least 40 different authors, but behind them is the main author, the Holy Spirit. 2 Peter 1:21 says,

> *'For prophecy never had its origin in the will of man, but men spoke from God as they were carried along by the Holy Spirit.'*

Behind each book of the Bible is the Holy Spirit directing the writer to write the mind of God.

As God is One so His Word is One. It is God's revelation to mankind and God's revelation is His Son Jesus Christ.

1. The Bible is a unity

Both the Old and New Testaments form essential parts of God's special revelation. Both have the same purpose, contain the same doctrine of redemption, speak of the same Christ. The morals in both are the same. If you could not commit adultery under the Old Testament then you cannot do so under the New Testament.

At the same time the revelation they contain is progressive, gradually God revealed more light. You may have heard this saying 'The New in the Old concealed and the Old in the New revealed.' The New Testament is a commentary on the Old. When the New Testament speaks of Scripture it refers to all the Old Testament, but Peter makes it clear in 2 Peter 3:15–16 that Paul's letters were accepted as Scripture.

2. *Many New Testament passages can only be understood by reference to the Old Testament*

The book of Hebrews is the best example. Here the author shows the link between the two testaments. As the book opens the author tells us that God spoke through the prophets, but now has spoken to us by His Son. The writer shows that the religion revealed in the Old Testament was the highest and best, but then goes on to prove that Christianity has replaced the religion of the Old Testament. Therefore he shows that the New was predicted in the Old.

John 1:29 says, *'Look, the Lamb of God, who takes away the sin of the world.'* Here is a statement that can only be understood by reference to the Old Testament. In Genesis, Abraham says to his son Isaac, who he is just about to sacrifice, *'God himself will provide the lamb.'* It was the lamb in Exodus 12 that was used to save the children of Israel. There is a link here with Leviticus 23:12 where a lamb had to be sacrificed, the lamb being without defect. This leads us to Isaiah 53:7 where we read that God's servant (who is Christ) was *'led like a lamb to the slaughter.'* These and many more verses give light to the meaning of 'the Lamb' in John 1. So in this example, New Testament teaching has been made clear by comparison with Old Testament references.

3. *We need to compare scripture with scripture*

The Apostle Paul does this in 1 Corinthians 2:13 where he literally says, *'with spiritual things, spiritual things comparing.'* This passage is all about the understanding of spiritual things. So here we have another valuable principle: one part of God's Word is explained by another. We look at scriptures side by side, and as we do this the harmony of the Bible is shown. This does mean that we need to know the Bible before we can begin to find the passages we should compare. When we make these comparisons we will see:

(a) The prophecy and the fulfilling of the prophecy.

(b) Types and their anti-types (more of that later).

(c) Revealed truth becoming clearer and clearer.

4. Use of cross-references

My first Bible was the Authorised Version. Down the centre of the page was a column with references and small letters and numbers linking them with different verses. Many of these were cross-references. Some modern versions have them at the foot of the page, others still keep the centre column. If I open my Bible at random I have Luke 15:24. Here two references are given, Luke 15:32 which repeats the same words *'was dead and is alive'*, and the other reference is Luke 9:60 which speaks of the dead burying their own dead. These cross-references help us in various ways and can be useful.

▶ Verbal cross-references

This is a reference that contains the same word or words as in Luke 15 above. We do have to be careful because not all verbal cross-references contain exactly the same words. These can be divided into **real** and **apparent**. **Real** means it is obvious because here the words are identical and they aid our understanding. An example would be 'soul' and 'spirit'. Both have a basic meaning of 'breath' in the Old Testament. **Apparent** references contain some words which are of no help in interpretation because the writer might use them in a different context. 'Save' is a good example. It can be used in a physical sense and in the spiritual sense. Thinking that any use of a word anywhere in the Bible is the same can lead us into all kinds of strange interpretations. This is where a good concordance comes in handy.

▶ Conceptual cross-references

This is when the same word or words are not necessarily there, but the same idea is. For example Hebrews 2 and

Philippians 2 discuss the incarnation; Romans 3 and Hebrews 10 are about the atonement; 1 Corinthians 15 and Revelation 20 are about the resurrection from the dead. These passages compared help us to gain better insight. A part might be missing from one passage but is present in the other.

▶ Parallel cross-references

Here we see one passage in a book being the same as a passage in another. The best example would be the four gospels. There are books on the subject of the harmony of the gospels. Just a word of warning here though, because we need to look at the context carefully. The cleansing of the temple in John 2:14–24 is in a different context from that in Mark 11:15–18. One is at the start of Jesus' ministry and the other at the end.

By comparing passages Paul's life can be pieced together from Acts and various passages in his letters. The Old Testament is full of parallel passages such as Exodus and Deuteronomy, Kings and Chronicles. Various Psalms also have parallel passages.

5. Old Testament quotations in the New Testament

One of the things that puzzled me as a young Christian was when I read a quotation from the Old Testament in the New Testament. I would check it out and compare the two and they were always different. I thought, 'Why did the New Testament writer change the quotation?' Later, as I read more, I understood that they did not change the quotation, but they were quoting from a different version of the Bible. The popular version of the Old Testament in the days of Jesus and the Apostles was the Septuagint, whilst most English Old Testament quotations are translated from the Hebrew Bible.

Comparing Scripture with Scripture is a very useful and valuable tool. A.W. Pink says,

> 'The Bible is somewhat like a mosaic, whose fragments have to be gathered by us and carefully fitted together if we are to obtain the complete picture of any one of its innumerable objects.' [1]

Note

[1] A.W. Pink *Interpretation of the Scriptures,* Baker House Book Company, 1972.

Chapter 14

A Look at Basic Rules (Part 1)

The next few chapters look at some general principles of interpretation. These principles will fit any passage of Scripture. The principles are standard guides which can be found in the more academic textbooks on interpretation. They are important and cannot be ignored.

1. The original language must come first

I remember being in a Bible study some time ago when the new paraphrased version of the Bible 'The Living Bible' by Kenneth Taylor had been published. Just one man in the room had a copy, the rest of us had the Authorised Version. A strong discussion started and it was all based on a verse in the Living Bible. No matter what anyone said, the man would not change his view as 'his' version said so and so. We must realise that it is no good getting upset about the various translations. What really matters is what does the original say?

Please don't be put off by this principle. Very few ordinary churchgoers know Hebrew or Greek and even less Aramaic. But with good books and a little hard work you can find out the meaning. An excellent aid for the New Testament is an interlinear Greek–English New Testament. Here the Greek text is set out and underneath is the nearest English translation. Remember there is no such thing as a perfect translation from one language to another. Also the word order is different in the Greek so the English words appear in a different order.

Something to know:
Interpretation depends on translation.

Many people still use the Authorised Version (King James translation of 1611). Others use revised versions. More modern versions are the New International Version, Good News Bible and New King James Bible amongst others.

Examples

(a) Think of the word 'atonement' in the Authorised Version, Romans 5:11. The Greek word here should be translated 'reconciliation'. In fact the actual word 'atonement' does not appear in the New Testament. Remember we are talking about the original language here – Greek.

(b) In Hebrews 7 (AV) we read of Melchisedek – this mysterious priest whom Abraham met. We read in verse 3, *'Without father, without mother, without descent'* which sounds very mysterious as if he just appeared from nowhere. In English 'without descent' is taken to mean 'having no children', but the Greek word is better translated 'without genealogy'. Melchisedek could have had children, but no list was available. We are not to think of this man as childless, there is just no record of any.

(c) Hebrews 7:26 (AV) says, *'For such an high priest became us.'* This sounds like Jesus becoming man, but dig into the Greek and we find it means 'to be fitting'. In other words we have a high priest who is just right for us – he fits our needs in every situation.

If in doubt – don't argue. Look it up in a good dictionary of Bible words.

2. Truth is revealed to humans

No one has ever seen God (John 1:18), meaning no human knows everything about Him. Because of this God had to make His truth available to us so that we could understand it. Therefore God spoke in human language. The truth is revealed to us through the culture of the Middle East. Unless we can understand God's truth it is meaningless to us, so for the truth to have meaning, it had to come in human thought-forms and relate to human experience. The term for this is *anthropomorphic* – quite a word! (*Anthrop* means 'in composition, man, human'. *Morph* means 'shape'. So *anthropomorphic* means 'of human shape').

Examples

(a) In Isaiah 40:10 we read, *'See, the Sovereign Lord comes with power, and his arm rules for him.'* We know that God does not have an arm because He is Spirit. But when we think of a human arm we think of strength so this is God's way of revealing that He is strong.

(b) We know that Christ is seated at God's right hand, but again God does not have a right hand in human terms. This is a way of us knowing that Jesus Christ is in the place of pre-eminence because that is the place of honour at the side of a king.

(c) Think of how God describes heaven. I think it is actually un-describable but God pictures it for us using all the most precious things of earth – gold, jewels etc. The fact that He says there is no death and no tears there helps us to understand.

Seisenberger says,

> 'We must not be offended by anthropomorphic expressions, which seem to us out of keeping with our

conception of God. It is with a well-considered design that the Holy Scriptures speak of God as of a Being resembling man, and ascribes to Him a face, eyes, ears, mouth, hands, feet and the sense of smell and hearing. This is done out of consideration for man's power of comprehension.'[1]

A note of warning here. Some people are far too literal and take this principle too far. They speak as though God **does** possess a body. We know the Lord Jesus does, but nowhere are we told that God the Father does.

Something to know:
God reveals Himself in human language.

3. Progressive revelation

We know King David was *'a man after God's own heart'* – yet he had many wives. We know Joshua was chosen to succeed Moses as the leader of the children of Israel – yet he led them into the most awful killings. We know Nehemiah was called of God to return to Jerusalem and re-build the walls – yet at the end of the book we read of him splitting up families and causing much suffering.

Have you ever wondered why? It has to do with the amount of spiritual light that these people had at the time. This principle is about the way God revealed Himself. It was not all at once, it was a gradual revelation. God took it upon Himself to reveal Himself to mankind. In a way we could say that in the Old Testament mankind was in childhood, but as we move into the New Testament man starts to grow up. The light God revealed is likened to lines that start together and gradually get wider and wider through time as more and more light is revealed.

Hebrews 1:1–2 tells us,

> *'In the past God spoke to our forefathers through the prophets at many times and in various ways, but in these last days he has spoken to us by his Son, whom he appointed heir of all things, and through whom he made the universe.'*

Here the writer is saying that the final revelation (the last bit of the light) came with the arrival of Jesus Christ. It's interesting to note that in the Greek text Hebrews begins with three adverbs. They tell us the way in which God spoke to Israel.

(a) The revelation came in an uneven way through the time of the Old Testament.

(b) The way God revealed Himself varied. God spoke in different ways and revealed Himself in different ways.

(c) The period of this revelation was in the distant past (the Old Testament).

This principle is important and it is good to remember Augustine said 'Distinguish the times and you will harmonise Scripture.'

No one is saying that the Old Testament is less inspired than the New, but that it contains less light – the fullness of the revelation came with Christ. Here is a clear revelation!

Something to know:
God revealed Himself gradually through history.

Note

1 Seisenberger, *Practical Handbook for the Study of the Bible.*

Chapter 15

A Look at Basic Rules (Part 2)

4. Being true to history

In John 3:5 Jesus tells Nicodemus that *'no-one can enter the kingdom of God unless he is born of water and the Spirit.'* This verse has caused many problems down the years. What does Jesus mean by water? Here are three ways of looking at the word 'water'.

(a) It means infant baptism – as a child is baptised he is born again.

(b) It means adult baptism – as a believer is baptised he is born again.

(c) It means the Word of God – mentioned in Ephesians 5:26.

Let us examine these things with 'being true to history' in mind. The first question to ask is: 'What did the words mean to Nicodemus?' I do not think Nicodemus had heard of infant baptism. He would have heard of adult baptism and we have to allow this possibility. But what about the Word of God? Asking our question gives us a clue. Nicodemus could not have read Paul's words in Ephesians because it was not written at the time he had the conversation with the Lord.

So what was happening at the time? Most of us know that water means cleansing. Something was happening down at the River Jordan. John was baptising with a 'baptism of repentance'. This view is the most true to history. John the Baptist had stirred the nation by his ministry and his emphasis on repentance. Water could remind Nicodemus of the Baptist's emphasis – in order to enter the kingdom Nicodemus needed repentance and the Holy Spirit. Titus 3:5 says,

> *'He saved us by the washing of rebirth and the renewal by the Holy Spirit.'*

A.J. Maas says,

> 'The true sense of the Bible cannot be found in an idea or thought historically untrue.' [1]

Some read the Last Supper into John chapter 6:53. Ask the question again: 'What did this mean to the hearers at the time?' The evening of the Last Supper was many months away so the people hearing these words could not have the Last Supper in mind as it had not yet taken place. Set the events in history.

It is good to remember that the Bible originated in history and can only be understood in the light of history.

Something to know:
Your interpretation must be true to history.

5. Understand interpretation and application

I used to ask my class to interpret John 3:30, *'He must become greater; I must become less.'* Each time students would volunteer to explain this verse to the class and each time they said, 'The Lord must become greater and we must become less.' I then asked, 'What was wrong with that interpretation?'

Eventually someone thought it through and realised it applied to John the Baptist and not to us. How easy it is to mix application with interpretation.

Generally there is one interpretation and many applications. There is nothing wrong in saying we have to become less and Jesus has to become more in our lives. But that is an application and not an interpretation. This verse refers to John the Baptist and him only. John had to become less – that is lose his popularity – and Jesus had to become greater in popularity, and that is exactly what happened.

What we often do is take a moral application as our interpretation.

Example

Someone leading the worship in our church quoted 2 Chronicles 7:14,

> *'If my people, who are called by my name, will humble themselves and pray and seek my face and turn from their wicked ways, then I will hear from heaven and will forgive their sin and will heal their land.'*

It was said that we must do this – humble ourselves, pray, seek the Lord's face, leave our wickedness – and only then would God hear us as a praying church. There is nothing wrong with that though, but again application is being mixed up with interpretation. This passage is about the Lord appearing to King Solomon and giving him a word of prophecy.

I fear this is a very common problem with preachers. They take most texts as if they apply to themselves and their congregation. It is looking at the Bible in a devotional way, putting self at the centre of the Bible. It might make for colourful and attractive preaching, but it is not good interpretation.

Something to know:
Do not mix interpretation with application.

6. Look for the clearest interpretation

If you come across two interpretations and both seem to be good as far as the principles go, but when you look closely at them one does not sound as credible as the other, the principle to follow is 'choose the more obvious meaning rather than the less obvious.' Choose that which is clear over that which is unclear.

It could be put another way, 'obscure passages must give way to clear passages.'

Examples

(a) 1 Corinthians 15:29 is an obscure passage and much has been made of this. There are many interpretations of the passage prompted by a desire to stick to an orthodox view of baptism. This is not saying proxy-baptism is scriptural, but Paul is referring to this as a practice of those who denied the resurrection. That is clear from the context.

(b) In Genesis 2:21 it says,

> *'So the LORD God caused the man to fall into a deep sleep; and while he was sleeping, he took one of the man's ribs and closed up the place with flesh.'*

The Hebrew word used here for 'rib' also means 'side'. So Eve was made either from Adam's side or his rib. Those who prefer side believe Adam was bisexual, and was divided into two sexes. The other view taking 'rib' speaks of the woman being built from a part of man to show their essential physical and spiritual kinship. The first stretches our belief, the second is the more obvious choice.

(c) Romans 10:18 says,

> *'But I ask, did they not hear? Of course they did; "Their voice has gone out into all the earth, their words to the ends of the world."'*

Colossians 1:6 says,

> *'. . . the gospel that has come to you. All over the world this gospel is bearing fruit and growing, just as it has been doing among you since the day you heard it and understood God's grace in all its truth.'*

These two verses give the impression that the gospel has reached out into the whole world. Let's apply this principle. If we take 'world' literally then we mean the whole world. But this is beyond belief because the gospel had only spread at this time around the Mediterranean countries. So we take this 'world' to be the 'known world'. Whilst we take a literal interpretation we do not take a strict literal interpretation of every word.

If we are looking for basic doctrines in the Bible we have no problem in finding clear passages. The doctrine of the resurrection is in 1 Corinthians 15; the doctrine of sin in Romans 1 to 3; the Deity of Christ in John 5 and Colossians 1; the relationship between law and grace in the book of Galatians. What is essential for salvation and our sanctification is clear in Scripture. We are not to go beyond what is taught in Scripture.

Something to know:
Obscure passages must give way to clear passages.

Note

[1] A.J. Mass, Exegesis in Catholic Encyclopaedia 5.

Chapter 16

A Look at Basic Rules (Part 3)

7. Let Scripture speak for itself

It is so easy to come to the Bible and read our own interpretation into it. Martin Luther said,

> 'The best teacher is the one who does not bring his meaning into the Scripture, but brings it out of the Scripture.'

We have two technical words for this:

(a) *Exegesis* – the basic meaning of exegesis is interpretation, one who interprets or expounds. Here we bring the meaning of the text out of the text.

(b) *Eisegesis* – this is just the opposite, putting our own ideas into the text and then saying this is what the text means.

The Bible only has one meaning; it is that which is found in the text. It is very difficult, perhaps impossible, for any person to approach the Bible without bias or prejudice. If we have been a believer for some years we will have collected our own prejudices, be it from our denominations or our favourite teachers. If we are new believers then we often bring to the Bible all our worldly thinking and that also colours our approach to it. But we are to determine the meaning of the Bible, not give it our own meanings.

Example

The Parables are a good example. People read all sorts of things into them. I once heard a preacher speak on the parable of the Good Samaritan (Luke 10:25–37). He talked about the donkey and said that the four legs and the tail stood for the Pentateuch – the first five books of the Bible. He then went on to say that the two ears of the donkey stood for the two Covenants – Old and New. As a young Christian I just sat there and listened. I did not know any better. Today I know he was speaking rubbish and it is a clear example of putting into the text something that is not there!

I think it was John Calvin who said 'Do not play with the Scripture as with a tennis ball.' We knock a tennis ball all over the place. Let us come to Scripture humbly and as willing learners.

8. Scripture is a unity

We must understand that the meaning of Scripture is one. When more than one sense is imposed the meaning becomes unclear and obscure. God is a God of order. He inspired His Word for a purpose i.e. to reveal the Lord Jesus Christ. The whole of the Bible points to Him – He is the central theme of the Bible. The message is one.

Some of the difficulties we have in interpreting the Bible are due to the large number of leaders in the early Church. We call them the Early Church Fathers. These date from the end of the Apostles (living around 100 AD to 400 AD). Unfortunately many of them interpreted the Scripture in a set way. They followed the allegorical school, which means they spent their time spiritualizing the Scripture. They were taken up with symbols and types. Therefore nothing was clear and straightforward, they thought everything had a hidden meaning.

Examples

You will remember the cord Rahab used in Jericho (Joshua 2:21); its colour was scarlet. The Early Church Fathers said this was a type of redemption because it was red. They saw baptism in every reference to water! And the crucifixion in every reference to wood! It is a shame that with some of their teaching the Word of God became confused and unclear.

Taking the Bible as a unity does not deny that figurative language is sometimes used in the Bible. Nor does it dismiss legitimate types. It is where the connection between the basic meaning and the expanded meaning cannot be justified that we are on very shaky ground.

9. Be willing to check with others

This is a very important principle because it stops us rushing off on our own without consulting those who have gone before. We can always check as we have access to so many good books. Using a dictionary, concordance, Bible atlas and all the commentaries can save us from so much trouble.

Think of the great doctrines of the Christian faith. Men today still go against them, making statements like denying the virgin birth of Christ, or His bodily resurrection. The tragedy is that these men are often in high positions in the Church.

The words of Charles Spurgeon are worth quoting,

> 'You are not such wise men as to think or say that you can expound Scripture without assistance from the works of divines and learned men, who have laboured in the field of exposition. It seems odd, that certain men who talk so much of what the Holy Spirit reveals to themselves, should think so little of what He has revealed to others.' [1]

I would like to give a word of warning here. Do not be a slave to one man – no matter what his standing in the Christian community. Look at various commentators and check with them all. We all have our favourite writers but it is good to check with as many as possible to see if we have an agreed interpretation. Remember we are interpreting the meaning of the text here and not applying it to the congregation.

Note

[1] Quoted by Bernard Ramm, *Protestant Biblical Interpretation*. W.A. Wilde Company, 1956.

Chapter 17

A Look at a Vital Question

In chapter 7 I gave an example from my lecturing days that is worth revisiting in this chapter. We had looked at a particular text in various ways, examined each word, checked the context and come to an agreement on what the text meant. One of the students said, 'I believe it means this!' When I asked what evidence he had to arrive at that interpretation, he replied, 'Oh, I just believe that is what it means!'

That statement got me thinking. He was looking at the verse of Scripture through his own eyes and based upon his own circumstances and feelings. That is what the text meant to him.

Here then is the Vital Question: **What does the text mean?**

You might think that is simple. After all that is what we are aiming for, to understand the Bible. But think about the student who 'believed'. He asked a different question. He asked: **'What does the text mean *to me*?'**

If you have a class full of students, or a Bible study group, or a church congregation and ask this question regarding a Bible verse, how many answers do you think you will receive? You could get a different meaning from each person in the group.

It is important to know that the meaning of the text of Scripture never changes. There is only one meaning – the one that the Author intended. We are dealing with a Book in which the Author – the Sovereign God Himself – is communicating to us human beings. The truth is unchanging, the purpose of God is eternal and utterly dependable. And to those who seek Him, God reveals Himself. I am thrilled when I hear the testimony of those who were given a Bible and read parts of it and have come to know the Saviour without any other person speaking to them – a real work of God's Holy Spirit, taking the words from the page and making them live.

So down through the years, ever since the Bible was completed and available for people to read, the meaning of the text became clear. We should always start with the question: 'What does the text mean?'

Is it always wrong to ask: 'What does the text mean to me?' No. Devotionally that is often how God speaks to us. As we read the Word in our quiet time we look to the Lord to feed our souls, to make His Word come alive so that we are built up in our *'most holy faith'* (Jude 20). Plain Bible study for the purpose of preparing sermons or Bible studies does not always feed our souls, but if we are able to give time to reading the Word and praying, this is the situation in which we will find the Bible speaking to us personally.

If we do not mix the two questions together, we will have no trouble knowing how to interpret the Bible. A good preacher tells the congregation what the Bible means, but does not leave it at that. Although it was written thousands of years ago, he brings it up to date and applies it to our modern day, what it means to us now and how we can live it out day by day.

Chapter 18

A Look at Types

Types and **typology** are not spoken of as much today as they were years ago and today are not often preached. Yet types are used constantly throughout the Bible. This was a method of preaching used by the Lord Himself. A type is something or someone that represents another thing or person. The anti-type is that which is prefigured by a type.

1. The key to types

The key is found in the little words that the Bible uses: 'as' and 'so'.

Examples

(a) Matthew 12:40:

> *'For as Jonah was three days and three nights in the belly of a huge fish, so the Son of Man will be three days and three nights in the heart of the earth.'*

The two words are easy to spot. **As** Jonah ... **so** the Son of Man. Jonah is the type and Christ is the anti-type. Here the Lord is using an Old Testament character to illustrate Himself and explain something that is going to happen to Him.

(b) Look at John 3:14:

'Just as Moses lifted up the snake in the desert, so the Son of Man must be lifted up.'

Jesus used this incident when Moses made a bronze copy of a snake to tell Nicodemus that He was going to be crucified (lifted up). The two words are clear to see. The bronze snake is the type and Christ is the anti-type.

These occurred in the Old Testament, and the anti-types in the New Testament.

The Old Testament is full of types. Not all are types of Christ but many of them are. The book of Hebrews lists several. You may have come across this little poem:

'The New is latent in the Old.
The Old is patent in the New.'

The Lord on occasions invites His hearers to find Him in the Old Testament e.g. Luke 24:25–44; John 5:39–44.

2. Something to note

Some say that typology is forced and not found naturally in Scripture. I think the verses above prove this statement untrue. But we must be careful not to stretch types to suit our own views. The best types are those found in the New Testament. As we interpret we must discover the underlying meaning of such events as the call of Abraham; Abraham sacrificing Isaac; Jacob wrestling with the angel; Israel being delivered out of Egypt etc.

We are not to look at every item in the Old Testament as if it were a type. All Scripture is inspired, but not all Scripture is a type. Also not every aspect of the type can be likened to the anti-type, particularly types that are of Christ Himself. Adam was head of the human race but when he gave in to temptation he was not like Christ.

3. Some human types

(a) **Adam**. Adam was constituted the head of the human race. Christ (the last Adam) was constituted head of the redeemed people of God. See Romans 5:14. Here we can regard Adam as a type of Christ. Adam was *'...a pattern of the one to come.'* See also 1 Corinthians 15:22 and 45.

(b) **Joseph**. He is not mentioned in the New Testament as a type, but we know that he was hated by his brothers and became the saviour of his people so he is a type of Christ. Acts 7:9–13 says, *'Jesus came to his own and his own received him not'* and John 1:11 tells us that Jesus became the universal Saviour.

(c) **Moses**. Deuteronomy 18:15–19: *'God will raise up for you a prophet from among your own brothers, like me.'* Compare to Acts 3:22–23; 7:35.

(d) **Melchizedek**. See Hebrews 5:6–10; 6:20; 7:1–25. He was clearly a type of Christ. Melchizedek was a priest-king showing the dual role of Christ.

(e) **David**. David was a great king who unified the country and overcame all his enemies. He is a type of King Jesus who *'must reign until he has put all his enemies under his feet.'* (1 Corinthians 15:25).

(f) **Prophet**, **Priest** and **King** are all types of Christ.

4. Some Hebrew feast types

(a) **Passover**. See 1 Corinthians 5:7, *'For even Christ our Passover Lamb has been sacrificed.'*

(b) **Sabbath**. This typifies the 'rest' promised in Hebrews 4.

(c) **Burnt offering**. See Leviticus 1:3–19. Christ died as the Lamb of God in complete dedication to God's will.

(d) **Grain offering**. See Leviticus 2; 6:14–23. Christ's perfect person is associated with His sacrificial death.

(e) **Fellowship offering**. See Leviticus 3; 7:11–36. Christ's death is the basis of fellowship with God and other believers.
(f) **Sin offering**. See Leviticus 4:1–5:13. Christ died as the satisfactory substitute to provide forgiveness of sins.
(g) **Guilt offering**. See Leviticus 5:14–6:7. Christ's death atones for the damage or injury caused by sin.
(h) **Day of atonement**. See Leviticus 16:1–28. The High Priest acted on behalf of all the people. Our Great High Priest acts on behalf of all who believe.

5. Some physical types

The New Testament shows us that two main 'physical' types are the **tabernacle** with its priesthood and system of offerings, and the **wilderness wanderings** of the Children of Israel. These are two areas from which much material is drawn by the New Testament writers. However, we should observe the following points when drawing from physical types:

(a) There must be a genuine resemblance in form or spirit between any person, act or institution in the Old Testament and that which answers to it in the New Testament.
(b) The type must have an ordination from God. In other words He meant to foreshadow something in the Old Testament in order to show us the better way in Christ.
(c) We cannot regard a thing that is itself evil as a type of that which is good. It simply does not make sense.
(d) The connection between the Old Testament type and the New Testament anti-type must be real, not accidental or superficial.
(e) Look in the New Testament to see how it treats the subject. Generally the New Testament deals with Christ and the fact of redemption. It teaches us moral and spiritual truths of Christian experience. Do not get taken up with small details, but look for the broad types.

(f) We are not to start looking for doctrine in types unless the New Testament affirms it.

(g) Always look at the context!

(h) Remember that the type is often on a human, lower, and often carnal level whilst the anti-type is higher and spiritual.

Examples

(a) Think about double types. The lion is a type of Christ *'the Lion of the tribe of Judah'* (Revelation 5:5), and at the same time applied to Satan: *'Be self-controlled and alert. Your enemy the devil prowls around like a roaring lion looking for someone to devour'* (1 Peter 5:8). The lamb is a type of the Saviour and also of lost sinners. Water means 'the Word' in Ephesians 5:26; the Holy Spirit 1 Corinthians 12:13; and regeneration in Titus 3:5.

(b) Note that one anti-type can be represented by many types. Christ by the lamb; lion; branch; reed, etc. The Old Testament is a deep mine ready to be dug so that New Testament truth is revealed.

Chapter 19

A Look at Parables

The Lord Jesus told many parables in order to get His message across to His audience. We often tell them to our children in our Sunday Schools. One of the basic principles of teaching is to move from the 'known' to the 'unknown' and that is what happens in the parables. A parable carries one important truth – not many truths like the message I mentioned in chapter 16. There are exceptions, but the general rule is that one parable contains one truth or lesson.

1. The meaning of the word 'parable'

The basic meaning of 'parable' is 'placing alongside'. It has to do with comparison. It is a method of illustration.

There are two words used for 'parable' in the New Testament:

(a) *paraboló* means 'to compare'. It is only found twice outside the gospels in Hebrews 9:9; 11:19. The comparison is in noting the lesson taught. The hearer must catch the analogy if he is to be instructed.

(b) *paromia* means 'a wayside saying, a byword, maxim, or problem'. Also found in 2 Peter 2:22 and John 10:6.

Dodd's definition of a parable is good:

> 'At its simplest it is a metaphor or simile drawn from nature or common life, arresting the hearer by its

> vividness or strangeness, and leaving the mind in sufficient doubt about its precise application to rouse it into active thought.'[1]

Parables differ from fables in that they are not trivial or fantastic; parables differ from myths in that they are not a creation of popular folklore. And parables differ from allegory which finds meaning at many points of the story.

People quote various numbers as to how many parables there are in the gospels, but it is generally accepted there are 35: 17 in Matthew; 2 in Mark and 16 in Luke. John 10:1–6 could also be seen as a parable because in verse 6 the word *paromia* is used.

I like Michael Eaton's definition best:

> 'A "parable" is any kind of teaching which in some way is not straightforward. It includes stories that illustrate, puzzling questions, any kind of riddle or saying that is amusing or surprising. "Parable" includes a saying that gets us to think and raise questions in our minds. A "parable" is the opposite to ordinary, uncomplicated, straightforward teaching.'[2]

2. Why did the Lord use parables?

Matthew 13 is the key chapter to understanding parables. This is repeated in Mark 4 and Luke 8. The key phrase is, *'he who has ears, let him hear.'* We all have ears, but not everyone hears. We know that because not all believe the gospel, and in the same way some Christians do not hear what the Lord is saying to them because their ears are often 'listening' to something else.

Parables are the Lord's way of teaching responsive disciples. Jesus used them in order to reveal the mysteries of the Kingdom.

At the same time as revealing the truth to those who want to hear, parables hide the truth from unresponsive hearts (see Jesus' words in Matthew 13:14–15 as He quotes Isaiah

6:9–10). The truth is hidden in order to test how a person will respond. The knowledge of the Kingdom was given to the disciples, but not to others who did not really want to know.

Because the language of a parable is simple, some think they are easy to understand. Yes, the story is easy to understand, but the meaning is hidden. They are 'earthly stories with heavenly meanings.'

3. Some rules of interpretation

(a) Parables only partially represent their subject. This is because a parable is a 'word picture' and cannot say everything about the subject being described. In each parable we find certain aspects of the Kingdom, but not every aspect.

(b) Determine the central truth of the parable. There are many details in some parables, but these are not the central truth.

(c) Find out how much is interpreted by the Lord. That is why Matthew 13 is important because here the Lord interprets the parables for us.

(d) Parables are **secondary** to direct teaching. Their main work is not proof, but illustration.

(e) Look at the context for clues as to the parable's meaning.

Example

Luke 15 is a good example. In verses 1 and 2 we read,

> *'Now the tax collectors and sinners were all gathering round to hear him. But the Pharisees and the teachers of the law muttered, "This man welcomes sinners, and eats with them."'*

The three parables that follow are the Lord's justification for eating with sinners. The shepherd in the first parable, the woman in the second, and the father in the third represent love, forgiveness and redemption in Christ. Lost sheep, a lost coin and the lost son represent the sinners and tax collectors that gathered round the Lord.

(a) Look at the introduction of the parable to discover its meaning: e.g. Luke 18:1–8; 9–14; 19:11–27.

(b) Look at the end of the parable to see the truth revealed: e.g. Matthew 22:1–14; 25:1–13; Luke 16:1–9.

(c) Sometimes the Lord's object is given at the beginning of the parable and then repeated at the end: e.g. Matthew 18:21–22; Matthew 18:35; Luke 12:15; 12:21.

(d) Compare the parable with any Old Testament association. Things like vineyards, fig trees, harvests and feasts have Old Testament references and can throw light upon the parable.

(e) Do not look for doctrine in parables. The tendency here is to look for our favourite doctrines in the parables and make them fit. This was not the Lord's intention. There **is** doctrine in parables, but this is not their primary purpose. Some of the parables about the second coming of Christ have been used to support various theories as to the timetable of the Lord's coming. The timetable is not what matters – what matters is that the Lord **is** coming again!

Notes

1 C.H. Dodd, *The Parables of the Kingdom* (third edition).

2 Michael Eaton, *Preaching through the Bible – Mark*. Sovereign World, Tonbridge, 1998.

Chapter 20

A Look at Prophecy

Understanding and interpreting prophecy is not easy. This is because different prophets used different words or terms to describe what they mean. Having a discussion with someone who uses different terms for things than you do is never easy.

In the Old Testament the root of the word 'prophecy' means 'to be called'. Prophets were people who were called to speak God's message under the influence of God's Spirit. To prophesy was a task the prophet could not avoid: e.g. Amos 3:8; Jeremiah 20:7. We read that *'the word of the Lord came to . . . '* hundreds of times in the Old Testament, but we do not really know how that word came. God used different ways to communicate with the prophets (see 1 Samuel 10:6; 19:20; 1 Chronicles 25:1–3).

Men were called prophets and also 'seers'. This word emphasised the means by which the prophet communicated with God. Exodus chapter 7:1 says,

> *'Then the LORD said to Moses, "See, I have made you like God to Pharaoh, and your brother Aaron will be your prophet." '*

Some light is shed upon this statement in Exodus 4:10–16 where Moses argues that he cannot speak and so cannot go to Pharaoh. God promises to appoint Aaron, Moses' brother, to be the speaker. Here then, we see that the word 'prophet' is one who speaks for another.

In the New Testament there are two basic words that are used: *prophéteia* meaning 'prophecy' and *prophétés* meaning 'prophet'. The first word carries the meaning of 'the speaking forth of the mind and counsel of God', and the second word 'one who speaks forth or openly'. The word 'prophecy' is used in the New Testament to mean,

(a) A gift (see Romans 12:6; 1 Corinthians 12:10; 13:2).
(b) The exercising of that gift (see Matthew 13:4; 1 Corinthians 13:8; 14:6; 1 Thessalonians 5:20).
(c) That which is prophesied (see 1 Timothy 1:18; 4:14; 2 Peter 1:20–21; Revelation 1:3; 19:10).

The main difficulty in understanding the word 'prophecy' is that the English meaning is 'telling the future or foretelling'. Both the Hebrew and Greek words mean more:

(a) Fore-telling, and
(b) Forth-telling.

So it is safe to say that any believer who speaks 'forth' the word of God is prophesying. Not many today are able to 'fore'-tell the future. There is much debate as to whether the Church needs prophets who tell the future, some say this has passed away. Who are we to say how God will use a person? One thing to note is that we have the complete revelation of God in His Word. Any prophecy would always be in harmony with the Word.

Something to note

(a) There are false prophets. 2 Peter chapter 2 and Jude make it very clear that in the Church false prophets had crept in and were doing their evil work. John gives us the formula by which we are to test the prophets and their spirit (see John 4:1–3). Today more than ever, we need to watch out for such people.
(b) Old Testament prophecy often had a double fulfilment. There was an immediate fulfilment and a long-term

fulfilment. The 'day of the Lord' is mentioned many times in the Old Testament – it has to do with judgement. When the Assyrians came against Israel and Judah, people knew it was the 'day of the Lord' as God was judging His people. Yet we read of the 'day of the Lord' in the New Testament (1 Corinthians 1:8; 1 Thessalonians 5:2; 2 Peter 3:10). This has to do with the end times when God brings in His final judgement.

The interpretation of prophecy

There is no easy way to interpret prophecy. We cannot turn to a formula and apply it to every prophecy. The language of prophecy is not always clear. Prophecy is like a picture painted with words and we do not always get the whole picture. Here are some guidelines:

1. Look carefully at the words of the prophetic passage

There are many proper names, events, references to customs and culture that we need to understand. Ask the question: 'Is the language a figure of speech, or poetry, or symbolic?' Prophets speak of the future in the language of past historical events.

2. Look at the historical background

There is much about politics in the Old Testament. Think of Isaiah and all that was happening between the nations in his day. To know something about this helps us to understand what he had to say. Jeremiah and Ezekiel become clearer when we understand the issue of the captivity of the nation (the Jews being taken into exile in Babylon for 70 years).

3. Do not ignore the context

Remember that the chapter and verse divisions are man-made and can mislead us. We ignore the context at our peril. Many a teacher has made a strong case by isolating verses, when really the verses before or after destroy his argument.

4. Note the way things are spoken

Things far into the future are sometimes spoken of as though they had already happened. Isaiah 9:6 for instance says,

> *'For unto us a child is born,*
> *to us a son is given.'*

Similarly, Isaiah 53:3–4 reads,

> *'He was despised and rejected by men,*
> *a man of sorrows, and familiar with suffering.*
> *Like one from whom men hide their faces*
> *he was despised, and we esteemed him not.'*

Note Isaiah says 'us' and 'we' as if the people were there and it was happening at that moment. This kind of language is known as the 'prophetic perfect' tense. It is used to emphasise the certainty of the predictions. Look at Romans 8:30. Here it is again speaking as if everything had already happened. A believer's position in Christ is so – everything is complete, but practically we will have to wait for the final fulfilment.

5. See two events together

Two or more events – which in their fulfilment may be separated by a long period of time – are some times foretold in one verse or paragraph as though they belonged together. For example, when the Lord read from the scroll of Isaiah in the synagogue at Nazareth in Luke 4:18–19 He was reading from Isaiah 61:1–2. The Lord stops reading after *'... to proclaim the year of the Lord's favour.'* He makes it clear that His mission is to proclaim God's mercy and favour. So the 'favourable year' had already come, but the rest of Isaiah 61:2, *'... and the day of vengeance of our God'* is still to be fulfilled in the future.

Some things to do

- Find out as much as you can about the circumstances in which the prophet proclaimed his message.

- Take care to interpret the prophet's use of figurative language correctly.
- Before making your final interpretation, look for parallel or similar passages that throw light on the one you are focusing on.
- Ask: 'Are the predictions fulfilled in the gospels or early Church?'
- Examine the way the Lord and the apostles interpreted Old Testament predictions. All spoke under the inspiration of the Holy Spirit so we should not neglect this method.
- Some interpretations by the Lord and the apostles are spiritual and not all appear to be literal.
- Wherever possible use the literal method.

Chapter 21

A Look at Figures of Speech

Life would be very dull without figures of speech. We use them all the time. Sometimes we know it and other times not. My father used to come in from work and say, 'I'm so hungry I could eat a horse!' The English language is rich with figures of speech. In appendix 6 of the Companion Bible[1] there are 181 figures of speech listed. I did not realise there were so many until I read this and had not heard many of them, but they are part of the English language.

Figures of speech relate to the form in which the words are used. Words are used out of their ordinary sense for the purpose of attracting attention to what is said. Figures of speech are always used for emphasis – so they are not to be ignored. Figures of speech are divided into three groups.

1. Figures involving 'omission'
2. Figures involving 'addition'
3. The alteration of a word or words

People who interpret the Bible in the literal way are often accused of ignoring the figures of speech. Feinberg says,

> 'It is not true that they [the literalists] require every single passage to be interpreted literally without exception.'[2]

As you interpret a figure of speech you cannot ignore the literal. The way to do it is to think about the literal application first.

Examples

(a) Revelation 5:5: *'The Lion of the tribe of Judah.'* Think about a lion. What does it stand for? Generally we think of the king of the beasts and of strength. The Lord Jesus Christ is both a king and is strong.

(b) Psalm 89:10: *'You crushed Rahab like one of the slain; with your strong arm you scattered your enemies.'* Here the use of the phrase 'strong arm' in the passage speaks of what God has done. We know that God does not literally have an arm because He is Spirit, but we think first literally about 'a strong arm' and then apply it to God.

When we come to Scripture and the language used by the Holy Spirit, we must remember the truth is literal while the words used are figurative.

Some common types of figures of speech

- **Allegory**. Teaches a truth about one thing by substituting another for it which is unlike it. An allegory is like a metaphor but much longer, and could be a whole story. (See Genesis 49:9 and Galatians 4:22–24 for shorter allegorical examples.)
- **Ellipsis**. Where a gap is left in a sentence through the omission of a word or words. These words are to be supplied by the hearer or reader from the context (Genesis 14:19–20; Psalm 21:12).
- **Euphemism**. A soft or moderate expression for a more direct and perhaps shocking one (Genesis 15:15).
- **Hyperbole**. The intentional use of exaggeration for effect. Saying more than you literally mean (Genesis 41:47; Deuteronomy 1:28).

- **Irony**. A method of being sarcastic or criticising or judging by seeming to praise or congratulate (see 1 Kings18:27 where Elijah taunts the prophets of Baal telling them to 'shout louder').
- **Metaphor**. A declaration that one thing is (or represents) another. A metaphor is a word picture. The words 'as' and 'like' are not usually used (Matthew 26:26).
- **Metonymy**. The use of one name or noun instead of another, to which it stands in a certain relation: i.e. crown for a king; wealth for rich people etc. (Luke 16:29).
- **Simile**. A declaration that one thing resembles another. The words 'as' and 'like' are often used (Matthew 7:24–27).
- **Symbol**. A material object is substituted for a moral or spiritual truth (Isaiah 22:22).
- **Synecdoche**. A form of expression in which the whole is spoken of for the part, or the part for the whole. It is the exchange of one idea for an another idea (Genesis 6:12; Matthew 6:11).

Some guidelines

▶ Be clear about the things on which the figures are based

The figures of speech in the Bible come especially from:

(a) The physical layout of the Holy Land
(b) The religious ceremonies of Israel
(c) The history of Israel
(d) The daily life and customs of the people of the Bible lands

Examples

(a) Psalm 51:7:

> *'Cleanse me with hyssop, and I shall be clean;*
> *wash me, and I shall be whiter than snow.'*

Cleansing with hyssop comes from the ceremonial purification of the Jews.

(b) Psalm 92:12:

'The righteous will flourish like a palm tree,
they will grow like a cedar of Lebanon.'

Here are two similes because of the word 'like'. To know about the palm tree and the cedar of Lebanon will help in your interpretation.

▶ **Find and focus upon the principal idea, not the less important details**

Examples

(a) Romans 8:17:

'Now if we are children, then we are heirs – heirs of God, and co-heirs with Christ, if indeed we share in his sufferings in order that we may also share in his glory.'

The metaphor 'heir' refers to the blessings which believers receive with Christ from their common Father. We are not to go on and make it mean more.

(b) Revelation 16:15:

'Behold, I come like a thief.'

It would be silly to stretch this simile too far. The Lord Jesus cannot be likened to a thief, He was referring to the suddenness with which a thief can come.

(c) When the figure refers to God, it only gives us a small picture of Him. God is called **light** in 1 John 1:5; a **rock** in 2 Samuel 22:3; a **fortress** in Psalm 18:2; a **sun** in Psalm 84:11; a **shield** in Genesis 15:1. All of these figures (and many more) give us some idea of what God is like for His people, but not one of them gives us a complete picture of what He is really like.

(d) When the figures refer to Christians it only gives us a small picture. The Bible pictures the redeemed as being:

dressed in garments of salvation, robed in a robe of righteousness, crowned with a crown of life and bearing the palms of victory. These figures do give us some idea, in part, of our future glory.

'A careful reading of the Bible will help us more than anything else to understand the figurative language of the Bible.'[3]

Notes

1 *The Companion Bible*, Oxford University Press.

2 Quoted by Bernard Ramm, *Protestant Biblical Interpretation*. W.A. Wilde Company, 1956.

3 L. Berkhof, *Principles of Biblical Interpretation*, Baker Book House, 1950.

Chapter 22

A Look at Applying the Old Testament

I find this a difficult topic! Just how do we apply the Old Testament in today's Church? We have seen that some of the earlier principles we have discussed stop us from interpreting passages directed to an individual or a group of people as if they were given to the Church.

We know all Scripture is inspired and has the same Author, but do we give equal weight to every part of the Old Testament?

One thing we know is that the Old Testament was the Bible of the early Church. The New Testament was not written and finally acknowledged as the 27 books we have today until about 400 AD.

Yet, the Old Testament is not Israel-centred but Christ-centred. In fact the Lord said in John 5:39,

> *'You diligently study the Scriptures* [the Old Testament] *because you think that by them you possess eternal life. These are the Scriptures* [the Old Testament] *that testify about me.'*

Most would give mental assent to this, but there are still disagreements about the use of the Old Testament.

Some people like to move others away from a Christ-centred Scripture to look at what they call the 'dispensations'.

These focus on God's earthly people Israel. Others emphasise the commandments that Christians are to obey. Many use the Old Testament in a devotional manner and this can lead to interpreting it as allegory.

Here are some general guidelines:

▶ Ask: 'How does the New Testament use the Old Testament?'

The way the Lord Jesus and the New Testament writers used the Old Testament must be our basic reference point. With modern versions, such as the New International Version, Old Testament quotations are inset in the text and so are easy to see. We know that the New Testament does not comment on every verse in the Old. Some Old Testament books are not quoted at all, but what we do have are references to the main parts of the Old Testament. Take these together and we have a thorough enough database for our approach to the Old Testament.

The early Church read it from the point of view that it was Christ-centred. If they did use it in an ethical way like in 2 Timothy 3:16, they still retained a Christ-centred focus. Nowhere do we find that the New Testament uses the Old Testament as a 'law book' to refer to. The early churches were united as long as Christ remained central. As time went by things were introduced from the Old Testament into the New Testament Church which caused division. For example, when some tried to impose a Jewish way of life on Gentile converts (Acts 15:1, 5).

▶ The Old Testament is interpreted by the Holy Spirit

As in all cases of interpretation, the presence of the Holy Spirit is our ultimate source of any hope of our proper understanding. The Holy Spirit inspired the Old Testament writers as He did the New. Because the Holy Spirit is Christ-centred (John 16:13–14) we can know that any interpretation that leads us away from the Lord Jesus or puts Him on the edge is not of God.

▶ The New Testament 'Law of Christ' is greater than the Old Testament 'Law of Moses'

The Old Covenant community was structured around a written revelation centred on Moses. The New Covenant community (the Church) is ordered by the 'law of Christ' as revealed in the writings of the Apostles and prophets – *'built on the foundations of the apostles and prophets, with Christ Jesus himself as the chief cornerstone'* (Ephesians 2:20). The Lord Himself made it clear that His 'law' is more severe than the old law. 'Murder,' Jesus says, 'is inward anger' (Matthew 5:22). Adultery is looking lustfully at a woman (Matthew 5:28). See how astonished the people were when Jesus finished this part of His teaching, *'because he taught as one who had authority, and not as their teachers of the law.'*

▶ Is the Old Covenant the same as the New Covenant?

The New Testament is clear. The two covenants are different. The first administered death, the other administers life.

> *'He has made us competent as ministers of a new covenant – not of the letter but of the Spirit; for the letter kills, but the Spirit gives life. Now if the ministry that brought death, which was engraved in letters on stone, came with glory, so that the Israelites could not look steadily at the face of Moses because of its glory, fading though it was, will not the ministry of the Spirit be even more glorious?'* (2 Corinthians 3:6–8)

It is the New Covenant that is binding on the Church. We must understand that the Old Testament is not the basis of the Christian Church. When the New Covenant came, a new basis of 'law' or 'rule' for the Church came with it. The Old Covenant was replaced by the dominion of Christ over His Kingdom (Matthew 16:19; 18:17–18).

▶ See the three different types of relationships between men and the law

This is highlighted in 1 Corinthians 9:20–21:

'To the Jews I became like a Jew, to win the Jews. To those under the law I became like one under the law (though I myself am not under the law), so as to win those under the law. To those not having the law I became like one not having the law (though I am not free from God's law but am under Christ's law), so as to win those not having the law.'

The Greek for the first group is *hupo nomes* – those under Moses' law: i.e. Jews. The second group is *anomos* – those without Moses' law: i.e. Gentiles. The third group is *onnomes christou* – those 'in-lawed' to Christ: i.e. Christians.[1]

We must be careful how we apply the Old Testament in the Church. Let us do it carefully, thoughtfully and prayerfully using all the rules of interpretation.

Note

1 Told to me by Jon Zens, Editor of *Searching Together* Magazine. Box 377, Taylors Falls, MN 55083 USA.

Chapter 23

A Look at Doctrine

Doctrine is the sum total of all the Bible has to say on any given subject. If we had an old Bible and a pair of scissors we could cut out all the verses on a doctrine put them together and there we have it – the doctrine! But it is not as simple as that! Famous men have examined it for us and organised the topics of the Bible into a system – we call this **systematic theology**.

2 Timothy 3:15–17 tells us the dual purpose of Scripture:

> *'...and how from infancy you have known the holy Scriptures, which are able to make you wise for salvation through faith in Christ Jesus. All Scripture is God-breathed and is useful for teaching, rebuking, correcting and training in righteousness, so that the man of God may be thoroughly equipped for every good work.'*

Its first purpose is to make sinners into saints – *'wise to salvation through faith in Christ Jesus'*. Its second purpose is to make those saints into mature saints. This is the maturity that Paul speaks of in Ephesians 4:13.

We know that the knowledge of God is expressed in the teaching in Scripture. This is called the *didaché*. As we learn and understand the teaching it changes our lives. Some say all you have to do is learn and give assent to the **doga**. Others learn and give assent to a **creed**. But throughout the

Reformation, the Reformers discovered that it was the Word of God that was central – belief in the Scriptures themselves.

See how the Lord stressed teaching

1. Jesus final command to His disciples was,

   'Therefore go and make disciples of all nations, baptising them in the name of the Father and of the Son and of the Holy Spirit, and ***teaching*** *them to obey everything I have commanded you. And surely I am with always, to the very end of the age.'* (Matthew 28:19)

2. When He saw the great crowds He had compassion on them.

   'So He began teaching them many things.' (Mark 6:34)

3. We have already seen how amazed the people were at His teaching (Matthew 7:28). And where did this teaching or doctrine come from? It came from His Father (John 7:16). What I find so assuring is that the Lord then went on to invite men to discover this for themselves (John 7:17).

If doctrine is not important why is the New Testament so strong on warning us about false doctrine given by false teachers? (Ephesians 4:14; 2 Peter 2; Jude). If you look above (paragraph 2) you will see the first profit of inspired Scripture is 'teaching' (2 Timothy 3:16).

We can be very thankful for faithful men who down through the years have put together the doctrine for us. It is doctrine that gives the Christian faith its quality and form. We might not agree with every single point but the major doctrines of the faith are essential for us. These are what bring us together.

The essential doctrines of the New Testament can be separated into two major sections:

- **The great doctrines of the gospel**: that sinners are lost; the death, burial, resurrection and ascension of Christ; justification by faith alone etc.
- **The great doctrines of Christian living: holiness and sanctification, church life, evangelism, etc.**

Here are some guidelines to interpreting doctrine.

▶ A Christian views the Bible differently

A born again believer has been changed. Having found the truth in Jesus Christ he is committed to it. He now comes to the Bible seeking the best possible explanation of what he believes. He sees in the Bible a record of the love of God, the grace of God, God's redemption and salvation given freely. The Bible is not a handbook of various beliefs.

▶ A Christian views Bible doctrine literally

You cannot have a workable system of beliefs if you spiritualise the Bible. This does not mean we deny that many truths in the Bible come to us through symbols, parables, poetry and types. But all the major doctrines can be understood by the literal approach.

▶ A Christian views the New Testament as the prime source of doctrine

Hebrews 1:2 makes it clear that God's final revelation is His Son: '*. . . in these last days He has spoken to us by His Son.*' In the New Testament we find all the Christian doctrines clearly set out. The life of the Lord Jesus is in the New Testament. All the truth of Christian living is found in the epistles. The full light of salvation came in the New Testament (1 Peter 1:10–12).

▶ A Christian views interpretation before any system of theology

The Bible itself is the divine record and not a theological handbook. As we correctly interpret the Scriptures we find we have a system of theology or doctrine. You will remember that it is **exegesis** (bringing the meaning of the text to the surface) not **eisegesis** (reading our own ideas into the text) that brings the rewards. Most of the damage done in the Church happens when bits of philosophy and Christianity are added together.

▶ A Christian views the Bible as sufficient

One problem in the Church today is that people have gone outside the Bible to supplement their doctrines and experience. The evidence must be in the Bible itself. This saves us from going off into flights of fancy. Sometimes we come across questions that we cannot immediately answer, but looking outside the Bible can only lead us astray. We can ask many questions about the future life: What will we look like in heaven? Will babies grow up? What will we eat? etc., but the Bible is silent on these things. You may have heard the statement 'The end justifies the means.' We cannot use this term when it comes to putting together our doctrine.

▶ A Christian views 'proof-texts' only as part of the whole system of doctrine

'Proof-texts' are the texts that we use to prove a doctrine. For example, you would not teach on sin without some of the verses from Romans 3. The Lord quoted verses of the Old Testament in His teaching. We quote the texts because we rely on Scripture. But in quoting proof-texts we cannot go outside the general rules of interpretation. A text cannot be taken out of its context. Teaching is not just a list of texts quoted one after another. Sometimes I have quoted a verse from the epistles and someone has commented, 'Oh that's only Paul's idea', giving the impression that Paul's teaching is inferior to the Lord's. But, the New Testament is made up of two **equal** types of teaching:

(a) **Dominican** – that is teaching by the Lord Jesus Himself.

(b) **Apostolic** – teaching by the other writers of the New Testament.

As the Holy Spirit is the author of the New Testament, we cannot give more weight to one part over another.

▶ A Christian views the faith within the revelation of God

Only what is taught in Scripture is binding upon us. Some churches may have rules and regulations but if they cannot be backed up with Scripture they are not to be made a matter of faith. There is a danger that the word of man is placed above the Word of God. We all need to be under the authority of the Word of God.

As we learn the great doctrines of the faith we find they bring stability to our lives. They help us to be clear in what we believe.

Chapter 24

A Look at Preaching

Every time a preacher stands up to preach, whether he knows it or not, he is using hermeneutics because he is interpreting the Bible to his congregation. Anyone teaching a Bible Class or Sunday School class is doing the same.

Everyone who uses the Bible to speak to others is a servant of the Word of God. We are not to be over it, but under it. The only reason we preach and teach is so that others might know the Lord and go on with Him, and that they in turn might tell others about the Gospel.

Before the days of the Reformation, the central thing in church buildings was the altar. Everything happened there. After the Reformation the altar was replaced by the pulpit. This came into the centre to show the importance of the Word of God. There is only one way a church can be taught and built up in their faith, and that is by clearly preaching and teaching the Word of God.

It is sad that some churches do not give the importance to preaching that the early Church did. Here are some verses which show the emphasis the Word had in the early Church:

> *'Just as they were handed down to us by those who from the first were eye-witnesses and servants of the word.'*
>
> (Luke 1:2)

This verse refers to the Apostles.

'But you will receive power when the Holy Spirit comes on you; and you will be my witnesses in Jerusalem and in all Judea and Samaria, and to the ends of the earth.' (Acts 1:8)

The Apostles were to be witnesses of the Lord Jesus.

'The elders who direct the affairs of the church well are worthy of double honour, especially those whose work is preaching and teaching.' (1 Timothy 5:17)

Note the emphasis on preaching and teaching for the leaders of the church.

'And the things you have heard me say in the presence of many witnesses entrust to reliable men who will also be qualified to teach others.' (2 Timothy 2:2)

Timothy had only one thing to pass on to others and that was the truths he himself had learned.

'Preach the Word; be prepared in season and out of season; correct, rebuke, and encourage – with great patience and careful instruction.' (2 Timothy 4:2)

Paul's instruction here is clear, *'Preach the Word.'*

I do not think we are free to preach what we want, but we are to preach the basic truths of Scripture. In some churches today the preacher can preach a whole sermon and never open his Bible.

Here are some simple rules to follow as you preach the Word:

▶ The preacher is a servant of God bound by the Word of God

What is your reason for preaching? Do you want others to look up to you? Do you want to be thought of as clever and maybe funny? Or do you simply want others to hear the great truths of the Word so they can be saved and grow as believers. I find it interesting that Paul tells Timothy, *'Until I come, devote yourself to the public reading of Scripture, to preaching and teaching.'* He is specific that the reading should be 'public'. Reading your Bible in your room is not public. This refers to when the believers come together. As the Word is read out loud and preached and taught it does its work. This is what the Holy Spirit uses in people's hearts.

▶ A preacher uses the Bible within the rules of interpretation

There is a phrase called 'poetic licence'. It means we can say things to people that may not be strictly true. In preaching there is no such thing as 'poetic licence'. Truth is truth. We never ignore context, and we are aware of what goes before and what follows our text. As we study we should apply the rules we have already covered and make sure our sermon is as accurate with Scripture as is possible.

▶ A preacher must make the Word interesting

Some people think that all they have to do is to stand in the pulpit and speak. Some do not even prepare and wait on the Lord to give them the message. You can usually tell when this happens. The message has no structure – it is just a talk. I like 'points' in a sermon, they are like hooks on which you can hang your clothes. They help people remember the message. There has to be life in a sermon and good illustrations to break the Word into small parts that people can understand. You cannot eat a whole steak without cutting it first into pieces – so a sermon should be prepared in small pieces.

▶ The preacher must make the Word relevant

One of the dangers of preaching is leaving the Word of God in the Bible where it was two thousand or more years ago. I have heard fine sermons which are not relevant to me sitting in the church wanting to be fed by the Word. So ask: 'What does it mean today? How does it affect the congregation now?' Bring the Word up to date. If your subject is obedience, then find ways in which Christians are to be obedient today. If your subject is suffering, think of ways Christians are suffering today and encourage them to stand firm in the Lord.

▶ A preacher must put some energy into his preaching

I can think of a young man who I have heard preach a few times who gives the impression he is not really interested in what he is saying. This is a great tragedy. I don't think we have to shout at the top of our voices all the time (unless we are in the open air with no microphone), nor jump around the pulpit. No! But we can put some energy into our voice. We can put imagination into our preaching. There has to be passion. I heard of a young preacher talking to a famous preacher about his lack of success in the pulpit and asking what he should do. The famous preacher answered, 'Try tears.'

Chapter 25

A Look at Quiet Times

George Müller (1805–1898) was the German-born founder of orphanages in Bristol. He is famous for his successful reliance on faith and prayer to pay his way. He once said,

> 'It has pleased the Lord to teach me a truth I have not lost the benefit of for more than fourteen years. I saw clearly . . . the first great business of the day was to have my soul happy in the Lord. I saw the most important thing I had to do was to pray after dressing in the morning and give myself to the reading of the Word of God and to meditate on it. Thus my heart might be comforted, encouraged, warmed, reproved and instructed.'

The one essential to Christian growth is that we read and study the Bible for ourselves. Not just to prepare sermons or teaching, but to feed our own souls. As we do this we interpret the Bible. I have already mentioned in chapter 2 the **devotional** way of reading the Bible. It is in our quiet times that we do this.

Most of the New Testament is written for Christians. So we have plenty that will help us to grow in our knowledge of the Lord and in holiness of character. The Bible has two aims:

1. To bring people to a saving knowledge of our Lord Jesus Christ
2. To help Christians become mature

As we read the Scripture we are to **read and feed**. The Word leads us into action. We may have to confess a sin, be led to pray specially for others, put things right with our fellow believers. Here is how we should read:

1. Meditate on the Bible

Meditation is thinking things over and over in our minds. Cows 'chew the cud' (chewing grass over and over). This is what we are to do with Scripture. Meditation is spiritually digesting the Bread of Life, feeding and building the 'inner man' of our spirit. Meditation helps to clear the mind because the Word has a washing effect on us, removing the dirt that we pick up just from living in a sinful world. Ephesians 5:26 speaks about being cleansed *'by the washing with water through the Word.'* Thinking God's thoughts purifies our thought life. Some recommend reading the Word aloud. This helps us to understand the meaning and fullness of a verse. There is great blessing in meditating on the Word of God (Joshua 1:7; Psalm 1:2–3; 1 Timothy 4:15).

2. Memorise the Bible

When I was a young Christian the Navigators used to make little packs that helped one to memorise the Word. It is as we remember the texts that the Holy Spirit can take them and use them, first for our own benefit, and then for others as we witness to them. What did Jesus say when He was tempted by the Devil after His baptism? *'It is written'* (Matthew 4:4). A soldier who uses a sword has to know the sword and know how to use it. We have the *'Sword of the Spirit which is the Word of God'* (Ephesians 6:17). As we come to each text, first we learn it then we have to retain it and finally recall it. Here are two good verses to start with both from Psalm 119:

> *'How can a young man keep his way pure?*
> *By living according to your word.'* (verse 9)

'I have hidden your word in my heart
that I might not sin against you.' (verse 11)

Here are some general rules for reading the Bible in your Quiet Times.

▶ As we read the Bible we must be guided by the general rules of interpretation

Some people seem to think that interpreting the Bible means they can do anything they wish with it – a kind of 'If I'm blessed by it then it is OK' kind of attitude. We are not to distort the Scriptures, but use them applying the rules that we have learned.

▶ The Bible is more a book of principles that a list of specific directions

There are clear references as to how we should live as a Christian, but what gives a good foundation and leads on to maturity is knowing the principles of the Bible. If the Bible is just lists of right and wrong behaviour then we could become very legalistic in our walk with the Lord. When we meet a situation in life that is not specifically covered in the Scriptures it is the principles of how God works that lead us.

▶ The Bible is about our inner spirit rather than outward religion

God looks on the heart (1 Samuel 16:7). Sometimes we test a person's spirituality by outward things – attendance at meetings, the way they dress, etc. But the Lord emphasises inward and secret things, such as prayer, giving, and fasting (Matthew 6:1–17).

▶ We should look for the spirit of the statement not always its literal application

No one wants to cut off their hand or pluck out their eye (Matthew 5:29–30). Surely what the Lord is saying is that we should not love our sins, but deal with them in a severe way. How many of us count the number of times we forgive someone? When the Lord said 'seventy-seven times' (Matthew 18:22), He was saying that we should go on forgiving because that is how God treats us.

► Commands concerning Bible culture must be applied in our own culture

Down the years commands in the Bible that pertained to the culture of the day have caused problems. Some have very strong views on hair cutting and the wearing of veils. Cutting hair in New Testament times was associated with prostitution. Wearing a veil was the sign of a decent woman. It is good that each church interprets these matters in the culture in which they live and the rest of us should not be judgemental.

► The Bible records things but it does not always approve of them

It is easy to think that everything in the Bible is approved by God. For example David's treatment of Uriah and the taking of Bathsheba is recorded, but God clearly disapproved of it (2 Samuel 11–12). Judas betrayed Christ. There is much cruelty recorded in the Old Testament, but this does not make it right for us to be cruel.

► Commands to one person are not the will of God for us

You will know by now that the correct interpretation of these commands relates to the person to whom they were given. Joshua, for instance, was called upon to kill in order to possess the Promised Land. We cannot apply such exceptional circumstances to our own lives.

Chapter 26

A Look at Promises

As a child in Sunday School I remember a chorus we used to sing:

> 'Every promise in the book is mine
> Every chapter every verse every line
> All are blessings of His love divine
> Every promise in the book is mine.'

As an interpreter of the Bible, do you think the chorus is true? Can you take every single promise in the Bible and claim it as your own?

The temptation is always to confuse interpretation with application. There may be a time in a quiet moment when God speaks to you through a promise, direct to your soul, and you claim it as your own. It becomes very precious to you and strengthens you in your walk with the Lord. God has applied His Word to your soul, but in general preaching and teaching we must be careful not to make every promise applicable to every situation. We must follow the rules of interpretation.

Here are some questions we should ask:

► Does the promise apply to everyone?

When the Lord said through Isaiah *'Turn to me and be saved, all you ends of the earth; for I am God, and there is no other'*

(Isaiah 45:22) He was making a general invitation to salvation to everyone. By contrast, the promises found in Ephesians 6:10–20 concerning a Christian's armour are for believers only. So here is the first thing we have to look for. Is the promise for everyone or specifically for believers?

▶ Does the promise apply to a person?

In Acts 18:9–10 we read:

> *'One night the Lord spoke to Paul in a vision: "Do not be afraid; keep on speaking, do not be silent. For I am with you, and no-one is going to attack and harm you, because I have many people in this city." '*

Here the Lord is speaking personally to the Apostle. This was a special promise to him to encourage him when he was going through a bad time in Corinth. The one thing we cannot do is command God to apply this to our situation. Genesis 12 is a very good example. God makes three great promises to Abraham, they are for him and his family, not for you and me (Genesis 12:2–3).

▶ Does the promise have a condition?

Often promises have a condition and the person reading the promise has to do something. God does His part if we do our part. Matthew 7:7–8 says,

> *'Ask and it will be given to you; seek and you will find; knock and the door will be opened to you. For everyone who asks receives; he who seeks finds; and to him who knocks, the door will be opened.'*

The condition is simple. We have to ask, seek and knock. I love James 4:8 which says,

> *'Come near to God and he will come near to you.'*

As we draw near to God we have the assurance He has drawn near to us.

▶ Is the promise for our time?

Many of the promises in the Old Testament relating to the Jews and their land are ended with the coming of the New Covenant. Some of the promises in Revelation are for the future at the end of the age. Even the promises in Revelation 2 and 3 are for specific churches. Some people treat the Bible as if it is magic. They pick out a verse and make it their divine guidance. This is not the way to determine God's will for our lives. It is by the daily reading of Scripture, interpreting it in a sound way, that will bring real, long lasting blessing. Short-cuts can deceive us.

As we come to the promises we must not only interpret them rightly, but accept the ones that are for us with faith. The Jews wandering about in the wilderness after they left Egypt *'... heard the message, but it was of no value to them, because those who heard did not combine it with faith'* (Hebrews 4:2).

Chapter 27

A Look at Versions

When it comes to the Bible, the English people are very privileged. They have had the Bible in their own language for hundreds of years. Following the Reformation which began in 1517, Martin Luther translated the Bible into German and William Tyndale (1492–1536) translated it into English.

He was not the first. John Wycliffe (1320–1384) was the first man to translate into English. This took 22 years and he was helped by many scholars. He used the Latin Vulgate Bible as the basis of his translation. It was all hand written and took ten months to copy out. When Wycliffe died, other men continued the work. Several copies of these Bibles survive today.

What was it that made it possible for William Tyndale's Bible to be so popular? It was printing! Johann Gutenberg (1400–1468) born in Mainz in Germany was the first European to print with movable types cast in moulds. In 1454 he printed his first book which was a Bible. So when William Tyndale finished his translation of the English New Testament it was able to be printed and so the Word was distributed quickly. What made this Bible so effective? It was translated from Greek texts making it an accurate translation, unlike Wycliffe who translated from a translation. Before he was killed for his work, Tyndale also translated the first five books of Moses and the book of Jonah. A man called Miles Coverdale finished the rest of the Old Testament.

So began a time of Bible translation. In 1611 what we know as the Authorised Version or the King James Version was published in London. This Bible was to become the Bible of the English-speaking world for the next 300 years. It is interesting to note that the Bible was never actually authorised by the King.

During the reign of Queen Victoria (1837–1901) a revised New Testament was published (in 1881 and considered by some to be the best) and an Old Testament followed many years later. After that it seems that we have had version upon version. Almost every few years we have a new Bible translation. The question is often asked: 'Which version is best?'

That is not an easy question to answer. I suppose my answer would be: 'What do you want to use the version for?'

▶ Use for general reading

It is good to just simply read the Bible. Some read a book at one sitting – while others take a little longer. For this a version that is easy to read is best. Kenneth Taylor's paraphrase *The Living Bible* is very easy to read. I also like Eugene Peterson's *The Message* very much for general reading.

▶ Use for preaching

It is important to be clear when preaching and to ensure that people understand what is being said. Therefore the same rule needs to apply to the Bible used. Some people can hear and understand the King James Version in its original English, but to most people it is difficult. So choose a version that is plain. I use the New International Version. Many of my preaching friends use the New King James Version.

▶ Use for study

Here it is important to use a Bible that gives the best reading of the text, one that is as near to the original as possible. I think there are two versions that are what we would call 'literal' – the Revised Standard Version and the New American

Standard Bible. These do not read all that well as they try to follow the original language word for word as far as possible.

If you can obtain a copy of the Interlinear Bible then that is even better for study. But I would not advise general preaching from these versions unless it is to a small Bible class where the people also have those versions and can follow. Whilst we strive to be accurate in our preaching and teaching, it is important that we are understood in plain language.

Chapter 28

A Look at How the Apostles Taught

One of the problems we have today is that preachers and teachers have to come up with something new every time they speak. This often leads speakers into all kinds of things that are not glorifying to the Lord. If we look into the New Testament we see that the Apostles did something different.

The secret lies in four words that were used by the Apostles as they taught:

1. Remind
2. Remember
3. Know
4. Don't you know?

As the gospel began to spread from Jerusalem into the surrounding countries, the evangelists Paul and Barnabas planted churches (Acts 13). They preached the gospel, taught the new converts and then moved on to start in another town. To some of these churches they visited a second time to strengthen the new believers (Acts 15:36). Later Paul wrote to some of these churches (nine of his thirteen letters are to churches). It is in these letters that we get the clue as to how Paul (and others) taught.

1. Remind

Jesus said a striking thing in John 14:26:

> *'But the Counsellor, the Holy Spirit, whom the Father will send in my name, will teach you all things and will* ***remind*** *you of everything I have said to you.'*

This is how the disciples could recall what Jesus said; they had supernatural help from the Holy Spirit who brought back to their memories the things the Lord had taught them.

In Romans 15:15 Paul says,

> *'I have written to you quite boldly on some points, as if to* ***remind*** *you of them again, because of the grace God gave me . . .'*

Leon Morris comments on this word 'remind':

> 'There is the tactful assumption that the Romans are knowledgeable in the faith and that Paul has not been putting novel teachings before them. He does not specify what it is of which he has been reminding them, but it will surely be the great truths of the gospel and of the way the Christian life should be lived.' [1]

Most of us who know the basic gospel truths do need reminding of them and this is what Paul is doing in his teaching. To the Corinthians he reminds them of the gospel in that well known verse 1 Corinthians 15:1; to Titus in Titus 3:1. Peter uses the same word in 2 Peter 1:12 and Jude in Jude 15.

2. Remember

The word 'remember' is similar to 'remind'. Paul to the Thessalonians says,

> *'Don't you* ***remember*** *that when I was with you I used to tell you these things?'* (2 Thessalonians 2:5)

He had taught them about the 'day of the Lord' so it was not new to them. He is now telling them to remember these lessons. It is interesting that Paul did not consider prophetic truth too deep for new Christians.

3. Know

The Apostle Paul starts off Romans 2:2 with the words, *'Now we know.'* Paul often appeals to his readers' knowledge. Sometimes he varies this to 'knowing' (Romans 5:3; 6:9; 13:11 – Greek text) This is a good way of teaching because it appeals to his readers' knowledge – something that they already know and can now bring to mind.

4. Don't you know?

This phrase is brought out well in 1 Corinthians where it is used ten times. Paul uses the phrase to introduce a statement that cannot be doubted. It occurs in 1 Corinthians 3:16; 5:6; 6:2, 3, 9, 15, 16, 19; 9:13, 24.

So we can follow the biblical example of teaching. Teach the people the basic truths of the Gospel (remembering that the Gospel is the whole counsel of God, not just the first invitation to come to Jesus). Then keep on reminding them of the things they have learnt. We are human and frail and we forget things. As we preach and teach we should make our preaching interesting and let the Word of God do its work.

Note

[1] Leon Morns, *The Epistle to the Romans*, Wm. Erdmans Publishing Co., 1988.

Chapter 29

A Look for the Future

In 1976 Harold Lindsell wrote a book called *The Battle for the Bible.*[1] This was followed in 1979 by a second volume *The Bible in the Balance.*[1] Both books are about the 'inerrancy' of the Bible. Put another way, the Bible is 'infallible'. Inerrancy and infallibility have the same meaning. When he was challenged about this he replied, 'I did not write the Bible. I only try to reflect what the Bible says.'

When you and I come to the Bible we have to decide: 'Is this God's Word or is it not?' After all, it is the Bible and the Bible alone that gives us the basis of our faith. Many churches have a sentence in their statement of faith that says, 'The Bible is the sole authority on all matters of doctrine and practice.' It is a pity that so many then choose to ignore that sentence and carry on as if the Bible does not really matter.

Today people are fond of using the phrase 'The Lord told me.' That is fine so long as what He tells you is in keeping with His Word, for God will never break His word *'and the Scripture cannot be broken'* (John 10:35). But when I taught at a Bible College for many years, students would use this phrase to try and persuade the staff they could do things that were wrong and not in keeping with Scripture.

I have tried to write a book that is not technical, written for ordinary people who want to seriously study the Bible and spread its Word.

As you have read this book I hope it has led you to look into God's wonderful Word and to accept it for what it is – God's inerrant Word. I think at times when we are dealing with God we can be too clever and forget we are the creatures and God is the Creator. So here are a few simple closing thoughts to guide us.

1. God is Sovereign

What do we mean by this phrase?

> 'To say that God is Sovereign is to declare that God is God. To say that God is Sovereign is to declare that He is the Most High, doing according to His will in the army of heaven, and among the inhabitants of the earth, so that none can stay His hand or say unto Him, What doest Thou? (Daniel 4:35)' [2]

God alone is Almighty, He has all power in heaven and on earth, no one can go against His will without suffering the consequences. To put it simply, God is on the throne!

2. God is faithful

> *'If we are faithless, he will remain faithful, for he cannot disown himself.'* (2 Timothy 2:13)

To be faithless means to disown Christ (v. 12). We are told God always remains faithful. This means He always keeps His Word:

> *'But whoever disowns me before men, I will disown him before my Father in heaven.'* (Matthew 10:33)

It also means He will keep His promises:

> *'Whoever acknowledges me before men, I will also acknowledge him before my Father in heaven.'* (Matthew 10:32)

The fact that God is faithful and we rely on this is of great comfort in every situation of life.

> 'The grace of God is always surprising. At the very point where you almost expect God to be vindicated and repay us for our faithlessness, He is faithful to us after all!'[3]

3. God speaks

In the third verse of the Bible we read *'God said'* (Genesis 1:3). Since then God has spoken in many ways, but His whole revelation is His Word. There is a series of Bible Commentaries called *The Bible Speaks Today* published by Inter-Varsity Press, Leicester. I am so glad that what God said has now been written down and we can have it in our own language and through it God still speaks today. We know and believe that what God has said is true and can be relied upon to save souls and to build up a Christian in his holy faith.

Continue to trust the Lord and His Word, to learn it, to practice it, and above all, to live it!

Notes

1 Zondervan Corporation, Grand Rapids, Michigan, USA.

2 A.W. Pink, *The Sovereignty of God*, Banner of Truth Trust, Edinburgh, 1961.

3 Michael Eaton, *Preaching through the Bible – 2 Timothy*, Sovereign World, Tonbridge, 1999.

If you have enjoyed this book and would like to help us to send a copy of it and many other titles to needy pastors in the **Third World**, please write for further information or send your gift to:

Sovereign World Trust
PO Box 777, Tonbridge
Kent TN11 0ZS
United Kingdom

or to the **'Sovereign World'** distributor in your country.

Visit our website at **www.sovereign-world.org** for a full range of Sovereign World books.